Walking the Tightrope

Talks on Meditative Development
with Pemasiri Thera

Walking the Tightrope

Talks on Meditative Development
with Pemasiri Thera

DAVID YOUNG

Buddhist Publication Society
Kandy Sri Lanka

Buddhist Publication Society
P.O.Box 61
54 Sangaraja Mawatha
Kandy, Sri Lanka
Website: http://www.bps.lk

First printing, 2005

Cover art: "Frozen"
(Egg tempera and aquarell, 1.65m. by 1.40m.)
by Junoš Miklavc (Slovenia) and Tena Rebernjack (Croatia), 2003

Cover design: Artplus, Belleville, Ontario, Canada

ISBN 955-24-0273-5

Young, David
Walking the Tightrope: Talks on Meditative Development
with Pemasiri Thera / David Young,
Kandy : Buddhist Publication Society,
2005 — 172 pp.; 21 cm

ISBN 955-24-0273-5 Price: $6.00 US

i.294.34435 DDC 21 ii. Title

1. Buddhist Meditation 2. Buddhism

Printed by Digital Teleprints - Kandy

The author dedicates this book to
the victims of the tsunami
that hit Sri Lanka on December 26th, 2004.

He also dedicates this book to
Mr. A.G.S. Kariyawasam
BPS editor-in-chief
who died on December 27th, 2004.

TABLE OF CONTENTS

Preface

Like many people, I often wonder what life is all about. Why am I here? What should I do? How can I find happiness? Where will I go when I die? Searching for answers to these timeless questions, I left family, friends, and work as a surveyor in Canada in 1990 and headed overseas. When I first began that trip, I admit that I didn't actually know I had these questions in mind. But through discussions with wise people I met on the road, it became obvious that these questions lay at the root of my search.

Europe, Israel, Egypt, Iraq, and India—each region of the world I travelled to was interesting and rewarding. But it was in the spring of 1991 while working as a volunteer for the Centre of Technology for Villagers, a grassroots rural development group in Thailand's Northeast, where I made my first real breakthrough. Encouraged by the local deputy postmaster, I visited Wat Pah Nanachat, a Buddhist forest monastery set up by Ajahn Cha for foreigners.

At Nanachat, there were English, German, and Canadian monks who had the same cultural background as I did and I could relate to them. The monks told me about the teachings of the Buddha, the four noble truths, and that craving was the cause for my suffering. "Suffering," they said, "is a fact of life. You aren't alone." Though these monks surely never thought there was anything particularly radical in what they were saying, I can't overstate the impact of their words. For the first time in my life, I heard that my craving causes my suffering. Revolutionary!

Returning to Canada in the summer of 1991, I worked again as a surveyor and eventually even tried nursing studies at McGill University in Montreal. I already had a B.Sc. in Agricultural Engineering. The summer of 1993, however, found me returning to Wat Pah Nanachat for further explorations of the Buddha's teachings as well as travelling to Copenhagen to get married. As usual, I was going in two different directions at the same time: monastery and matrimony. By 1995, I was divorced, out of nursing, and back to surveying. In the fall of 1997, with debts paid and money in the bank, I left with an American monk for Sri Lanka.

Sri Lanka is a very friendly country. It also has a lot of people working hard at practising the teachings of the Buddha. When the practitioners I met found out that I had travelled to Sri Lanka to learn more about the Buddha's teachings, there was no shortage of advice. Many of them, including Bhikkhu

Bodhi, told me, "Pemasiri Thera can help you. Go and see him." Perhaps the smartest decision I have ever made in my life, I went to see Pemasiri Thera at his meditation centre. He welcomed me with open arms and a great big smile, and I stayed for about a year.

A generous person, doing whatever he can to help people, Pemasiri Thera was always available for talks. Sometimes it was only Pemasiri Thera, a translator, and myself. While at other times, I joined group talks. One of us asked Pemasiri Thera a question and without fail he responded with sensible and at times quite surprising answers. Recognising that I wasn't retaining the vast majority of what he said, I began tape-recording our talks. By the time I headed back to Canada in 1999, I had a shoebox full of tapes.

To further my understanding, I transcribed the tapes and then selected a small fraction of the transcriptions for the heart of a book. Pemasiri Thera supported me in this undertaking. He knew that I would learn about the teachings of the Buddha by writing about them. Once I got into writing, however, it was clear that to write a book I had to do more than transcribe tapes. Being a surveyor and not a writer, I didn't know the first thing about putting a book together.

To create the best book I could, I read about the art of writing, consulted with writers, and took a college course in sentence patterns. I quickly discovered the spoken word is different from the written word: grammar is vital in written sentences, paragraphs must flow logically, and books involve a lot of planning because they have so many different elements. Since I am still learning about these things, I don't consider myself a writer.

I am also definitely not a Buddhist scholar. My background is Christian. When I began this project, I knew little about the Buddha's teachings and the Pali[1] meditation terms. I still don't speak Sinhalese. Pemasiri Thera, on the other hand, has a deep understanding of the Buddha's teachings, uses Pali terms constantly, and speaks only in Sinhalese. Consequently, we needed translators to communicate. And though Pemasiri Thera only uses translators who are highly competent, it is difficult, if not impossible, to completely render all the concepts and words of one language into another language. In addition, the translators had to evaluate what Pemasiri Thera intended to get across to me as well as evaluate my ability to comprehend. I thank the translators for exerting great effort in performing these tasks.

After I transcribed the teachings, I felt that I hadn't fully comprehended what Pemasiri Thera was trying to get across and I sought out clarification from monks and meditators, as well as staff at the Pali Text Society (PTS) and the Buddhist Publication Society (BPS). I also researched PTS and BPS material, and various Buddhist websites. Both the PTS and the BPS generously granted permission to use their material. Their terminology for Pali terms and meditation concepts is used throughout the book.

During the book's closing stages of creation, more than a dozen readers gave me constructive criticism, six editors corrected the text, and some friends helped with the design. It was at this point that I inserted at the beginning of each chapter excerpts from suttas of the Pali Canon; Pemasiri Thera recommended the suttas. Finally, not a bit of this book would have been possible without the financial and emotional support of family and friends.

Choosing the title and the subtitle for the book—*Walking the Tightrope: Talks on Meditative Development with Pemasiri Thera*—was easy. Pemasiri Thera uses the simile of walking on a tightrope to illustrate the practice of meditative development: both the tightrope walker and the meditator must pay very good attention to their mental and physical actions, as both situations are dangerous and precarious. As to the subtitle, the book contains many of the talks I enjoyed with Pemasiri Thera, and these talks were about meditative development. The term meditative development—Bhikkhu Bodhi's rendering for the Pali term *bhāvanā*, which Pemasiri Thera used—was chosen because it points to a mental and physical engagement in a dynamic process, and saves confusion with the familiar term of meditation.

Differentiating meditative development from meditation is important because many of us have fixed ideas of what meditation is all about and what it means to meditate. For Pemasiri Thera, engaging in meditative development is synonymous with the development of wisdom. It is to be practised all day and every day, and not just on special occasions, such as when we sit in one posture for an extended period of time. Pemasiri Thera considers all aspects of our lives opportunities for the practice of meditative development.

The more I got to know Pemasiri Thera, the more I understood why some people, as a compliment, call him a dinosaur: he comes from another place and time. This is a place where people are ethical, wisdom is developed, and the teachings of the Buddha are valued. A rarity in our modern times, Pemasiri Thera lives in a way that is almost extinct. He is an expert in the art of meditative development.

"Seeing things as they really are," said Pemasiri Thera, "is the purpose of meditative development." Taking me on as a student, Pemasiri Thera patiently and repeatedly brought me around to seeing for myself how I was thinking and behaving. It wasn't a pretty sight. I saw that my judgements, criticisms, and expectations resulted in a lot of suffering, for everyone.

Pemasiri Thera never told me what I should do to be happy. Instead, he gave me the Buddha's framework for evaluating situations and choosing wise courses of action. "When we have wisdom," said Pemasiri Thera, "we also have kindness and compassion." All wise people have come to the same conclusion. Some call it understanding the true nature of existence, while others call it unselfish love.

Walking the Tightrope is in essence a book about mental health. In it, Pemasiri Thera puts to rest many of the questions that drove me to travel the world. And with apologies for sounding a bit corny, Pemasiri Thera not only changed my life, but he gave me a life where one didn't exist. He showed me how to live in a meaningful way. This is a priceless gift.

In gratitude and respect,

David Young
Sumathipāla Na Himi Senasun Arana
Kanduboda, Sri Lanka, 2005

Websites and Texts Used

1. **Primary Websites:**

   http://www.accesstoinsight.org/
   http://metta.lk/
   http://www.ubakhin.com/ledi/

2. **Primary Texts:**

Bodhi, Bhikkhu, *The Noble Eightfold Path: Way to the End of Suffering*, second revised edition, Kandy: BPS, 1994.

Ñāṇamoli, Bhikkhu, *A Pali-English Glossary of Buddhist Technical Terms*, second edition, Kandy: BPS, 1998.

Ñāṇamoli, Bhikkhu, and Bhikkhu Bodhi, translation, *The Middle Length Discourses of the Buddha: A Translation of the Majjhima Nikāya*, second edition, Somerville: Wisdom Publications, 2001.

Nyanaponika Thera, *The Heart of Buddhist Meditation: A handbook of mental training based on the Buddha's way of mindfulness*, first BPS edition, Kandy: BPS, 1992.

Nyanatiloka Thera, *Buddhist Dictionary: Manual of Buddhist Terms and Doctrines*, fourth revised edition, Kandy: BPS, 1980.

Rhys Davids, T.W., and Stede, W., *The Pali Text Society's Pali-English Dictionary*, first edition, London: PTS, 1923.

Soma Thera, *The Way of Mindfulness: The Satipatthana Sutta and Its Commentary*, fourth printing, Kandy: BPS, 1975.

Walshe, Maurice, translation, *The Long Discourses of the Buddha: A Translation of the Dīgha Nikāya*, first Wisdom edition, Somerville: Wisdom Publications, 1996.

3. **Secondary Texts:**

Ñāṇamoli, Bhikkhu, translation, *The Path of Purification: Visuddhimagga*, by Bhadantācariya Buddhagosa, fifth edition, Kandy: BPS, 1991.

Narada Thera, *The Buddha and His Teachings*, second revised edition, Kandy: BPS, 1997.

Pa-Auk Sayadaw, *Knowing and Seeing*, second revised edition Kuala Lumpur: WAVE Publications, 2003.

Piyadassi Thera, *The Buddha's Ancient Path*, first edition, Kandy: BPS, 1974.

Weragoda Sarada Maha Thero, translation, *Treasury of Truth, Illustrated Dhammapada*, first edition, Taipei: The Corporate Body of the Buddha Educational Foundation, 1993.

List of Abbreviations

A.	Aṅguttara Nikāya
S.	Saṃyutta Nikāya
Sn.	Sutta Nipāta
Vism.	Visuddhimagga
D.	Dīgha Nikāya
M.	Majjhima Nikāya
Dh.	Dhammapada

Part 1

General Talks with Pemasiri Thera

"Meditator"
(Paper and pencil, 18cm. by 18cm.)
Tena Rebernjak (Croatia) (2004)

Venerable Ānanda said to the Buddha, "This is half of the spiritual life, lord: having admirable people as friends, companions, and colleagues."

"Don't say that Ānanda," said the Buddha. "Don't say that. Having admirable people as friends, companions, and colleagues is actually the whole of the spiritual life."

Upaddha Sutta[2]

1 Introduction

PEMASIRI THERA: Hello. Cup of tea?

DAVID: Please.

What shall we talk about?

For developing my practice of meditation, how useful are books?

Of course, the Buddha's teachings are in many books, and you will make some progress by reading and using them. But if you want your practice to go beyond its initial stages of development, a teacher is essential. The knowledge you gain from reading only supports your practice. When you work with a good teacher, you will progress on a constant daily basis.

Since you rarely take students, why are you teaching me?

You have the need and want for a teaching. There are many people who come and ask for a teaching, but have no genuine interest. These people often know the teachings of the Buddha very well, but forget to apply their knowledge when they contact an object with their senses. I feel you are genuinely interested in learning and applying the teachings of the Buddha. In your case, there might be hope and this encourages me.

You have been teaching me for half a year now. Would you explain a little about your methods of teaching?

When we first met, you knew very little about the teachings of the Buddha. We talked about everyday things and got to know each other. I asked how you were, what you were doing, and why you came to visit. We talked about things that related to your life. When you first arrived, I did not give you any weighty lectures on the *dhamma*. No. Nor did I sit you down and preach my core principles and methods of meditation. If I had, you would have just got fed up and left. Instead, I tried to be patient. Mostly listening, I tried to assess your attitudes, to a certain extent your mentality, and whether or not you had any real intention to learn the *dhamma*. I also tried to settle on the most suitable method for getting the *dhamma* across to you. Then, little by little, our discussions broadened to encompass more complicated and difficult topics. This is how the *dhamma* must be approached.

In the suttas, you find the phrase *saraṇīya-kathā*, which means remembering general talk. When a newcomer visited the Buddha, the Buddha began their conversation with general questions: "Are you hungry?" "Where are you from?" and "What do you want?" That was his way. After a general conversation with the visitor, the Buddha turned the conversation towards *dhamma-kathā*, which means talk of the *dhamma*. The Buddha only gradually introduced the *dhamma*. He did not immediately deliver sermons.

For example, if a rancher visited, the Buddha might ask: "How are you?" "How are your cattle?" and "What are your methods for tending to cattle?" Listening carefully to the rancher's answers, the Buddha obtained useful information about the rancher's life. The Buddha may well have said to the rancher: "Yes, that is a good method for tending to the cattle. I have a similar method for tending to the *saṅgha*."

As teachers, we try to use the same approach as the Buddha. We stop. We listen carefully to what the person is saying. Then, after having some general conversation, we gradually introduce the *dhamma*. It is difficult to discuss profound aspects of *dhamma* when we first meet people. It is inappropriate to approach a person just with *dhamma*. The Mahāsihasenapati Sutta of the Aṅguttara Nikāya is a good sutta to read.

When teachers talk with students, questions are answered in the same way they are asked. If a person asked the Buddha "how," the Buddha answered how this and that happens. If a person asked "why," the Buddha answered why this and that happens. If you had asked the Buddha a question about your eyeglasses, the Buddha would have used your eyeglasses to answer your question. He always started conversations with a very close relationship.

To the person?

Yes. In the suttas, you will find many accounts of how he instructed people in the *dhamma*. For instance, the Buddha went many times to one man's home because the Buddha saw that this man could benefit from his teachings. It was out of great compassion that the Buddha went to see this man. At first, however, the man was not at all happy to be visited by the Buddha.

"Hey," the man grumbled. "Why do you visit my home every day? I will tell you. You come here again and again because my food is so good and you like it. You are greedy. You come here day after day to get my good food. Again and again you come."

"You are right," said the Buddha. Then, using the same theme as the man, the Buddha added: "Again and again I come to visit you."

With the passing of days and weeks, the man relaxed: "I'm now glad that you visit me, again and again."

Because the man kept using the phrase *again and again,* the Buddha also used the phrase *again and again.* "Do you know what else happens again and again?" said the Buddha.

"Please tell me," said the man.

"Again and again," said the Buddha, "the rain falls. Again and again, farmers cultivate; again and again, farmers sow seeds; again and again, farmers harvest; again and again, beggars beg; again and again, people are generous; again and again, the calf goes to its mother for milk; again and again, we are born; again and again, we grow old; again and again, we die. In this world, all these things happen again and again."

"I know about these things," said the man. "There is nothing unusual about their occurrence."

"But do you know," asked the Buddha, "how to stop the cycle of again and again?"

"No," said the man. "I don't."

The man was now receptive to learning the *dhamma*. "When you understand," said the Buddha, "that all these phenomena are subject to suffering, are impermanent, and insubstantial, then you understand the true nature of existence, and there is no again and again for you. There is no again and again birth, there is no again and again old age, and there is no again and again death."

"Excellent," said the man. Insight arose and he attained path knowledge. This was the way the Buddha taught the *dhamma*.

Good story.

In another story, the Buddha visits a farmer who also had the potential to benefit from his teachings, and, although the farmer was very intelligent and capable, he was very proud. Out of great compassion, the Buddha went to see him.

On the first morning, the farmer was organising his workers to prepare his paddy field for cultivation. When the farmer saw the Buddha, he cursed: "Oh! Shaven-head. Get lost. Go away from here." The Buddha remained serene.

"You've ruined my whole day," said the farmer. "Why did you come here?"

"I came just to see what you are doing," said the Buddha.

The farmer was irritated. "I am trying to prepare my field for cultivation."

"I see," said the Buddha. "That is good." And the Buddha returned to the *vihāra*.

On the next day, the Buddha visited again.

"What are you doing?" asked the Buddha again.

"Today," said the farmer, "I am ploughing."

On the third day, the Buddha went yet again to the field.

"What are you doing?" asked the Buddha.

"Today," said the farmer, "I am levelling my field with water."

"Good," said the Buddha. "Very nice."

On the following day, the farmer was sowing the rice, and the conversation continued as it had on previous days. Every morning for three months, the Buddha went to the paddy field and their meetings became routine. When the farmer went to the paddy field, the Buddha also went to the paddy field. As time passed, the farmer stopped hating the Buddha and in fact started to like him. Intelligent and wise, the Buddha was a person the farmer could talk to. The Buddha's company was a welcome break from supervising the work and workers. The Buddha and the farmer developed a close friendship.

Eventually the crop matured and it was beautiful. Plants golden with their heads fully laden, both men were happy to see how the crop had grown and matured. It was now the end of the growing season and the crop was ready for harvest.

"For nearly three months," said the farmer, "you have visited me. You are a fine companion and, even though you haven't given me anything, I want to share the coming harvest with you. I want to offer half of it to you."

"Very good," said the Buddha. The Buddha accepted the farmer's generous offer and returned to the *vihāra*.

That very night, a heavy rainstorm flooded and destroyed the farmer's whole crop of rice. On the following day, the Buddha went as usual to visit the farmer, but for the first time in three months the farmer was not in the field. The Buddha walked up to the farmer's home, where he found the farmer in bed, very sad.

"Why are you so sad?" asked the Buddha.

"I am sad, not because I lost the harvest, but because yesterday I promised to give you half and now I cannot give it to you."

"*Taṇhāya jāyatī sōkō*," the Buddha told the farmer. "*Taṇhāya jāyati bhayaṃ, taṇhāya vippamuttassa, n'atthi soko, kuto bhayaṃ.*" This *gāthā* translates as: "From craving, grief and fear are born; for the person who is free from craving, there is no grief or fear." Reciting this *gāthā* is good for you too.

Though the farmer was an intelligent man, when he first met the Buddha, he simply was not listening to what the Buddha said about the nature of craving or anything to do with *dhamma*. At first, the farmer told the Buddha: "Get lost shaven-head. Don't bother me. I am very busy. I have many things to do. I have to feed and care for my family, inspect my fields, and supervise my workers. I have no time to listen to you or to your *dhamma*."

That is a common answer.

Yes. The Buddha had to keep going back to the paddy field until the farmer was receptive to hearing the *dhamma*. The Buddha spent three months visiting this one person because he knew it would take that much time and effort. The Buddha had the wisdom to know how to approach the farmer. The Buddha had the wisdom to give *dhamma* in the appropriate way.

As each and every person has his or her own individual way of learning, a good teacher always employs a number of different approaches to the *dhamma*. The teaching must be on an individual basis. One specific approach, one standard blueprint, in teaching the *dhamma* is inadequate. Sometimes the Buddha approached people quite softly and gently. In the case of the farmer who was sad because his crop was destroyed, the Buddha was merely a good friend.

Did the farmer attain some liberation?

Yes. After the Buddha explained the *gāthā*, the farmer attained path knowledge. This is why the Buddha visited the farmer for three months. When the Buddha looked through the world, he saw that the man had the potential to benefit from his teachings.

What is *dhamma*?

Strictly speaking, what the Buddha taught is neither philosophy nor religion, and definitely neither abstract nor ritualistic. His teachings are a practical way of living that leads to our release from suffering. Existing only briefly, to be a human being in a period of a Buddha's teaching is a rare occurrence. We have to grasp this opportunity to see objects in their entirety, as well as to see both the wholesome and the unwholesome. The Buddha's teachings are a way of being skilful.

Once upon a time, there was a poor elderly woman who ran a roadhouse. As part of her operation, she owned many horses, one of which was very skilful. And though doing what she could to give her horses the best possible care, she could only give them low quality feed because she lacked the money to buy the higher quality.

One day, a rich merchant with many ordinary horses came by to spend the night. When the merchant tried to put his ordinary horses in the stable alongside the skilful horse, his ordinary horses became afraid of the skilful horse and drew back. They balked. "I am curious about one of your horses," said the merchant. "Is there something special about one of them?"

"Yes," said the poor woman. "There is one particularly skilful horse."

"Can I buy it?"

"Perhaps."

Agreeing upon a price, the woman sold the merchant the horse. But, when the merchant tried to take the skilful horse from the woman's stable, the horse refused to leave. "The merchant needs to pay more money for me," thought the horse. "I will stay put until he pays more."

Somehow, the woman and the merchant figured out why the skilful horse was refusing to leave. The merchant then gave the woman more money, and the horse left with the merchant. In the merchant's stable, the merchant tried to give the horse the same low quality feed that the poor woman had given it, but the horse refused to eat it. "Why," thought the horse, "should I eat rubbish when this rich merchant can easily afford to give me high quality feed?" The merchant was a smart man. Realizing what the horse required, the merchant gave it the higher quality feed.

The poor woman, the merchant, the ordinary horses, and the skilful horse—each character of the story acted according to the wholesomeness of their mental states. The skilful horse did not hold out for a higher price just to please the lady. It simply acted skilfully, saw its world clearly and acted without expectations. Because the elderly woman lacked the money to provide high quality feed, the horse did not expect her to provide high quality feed. It was satisfied with what she could afford. It is always important to see both the wholesome as well as the unwholesome. Like the skilful horse, when we see the unwholesome, we reject it. And when people engage in unwholesome activities, we don't join them. Keeping the company of good friends is very important.

It is difficult to find a good friend.

No. It is not difficult. Clear comprehension is a good friend.

But there are so many unkind people.

There is no need to be too concerned about what other people say and do. We have got used to turning our minds outwards, watching what's going on externally. It's a bad habit. There is really no need to be looking at others.

"Abide," said the Buddha, "constantly looking at oneself." The more we look at ourselves, the better off we'll be. It is through the practice of meditative development, *bhāvanā* in the Pali language, that we come to know our strengths and weaknesses. Knowing the fundamentals of meditative development is very important, but it is a topic that generally needs to be discussed at great length. It can take six months to learn the fundamentals.

I am interested.

Right from the beginning, it's important to know that meditative development means reducing the five hindrances, *nīvaraṇa*:

1. Excitement of sensual pleasures, *kāma-cchanda*
2. Ill will, *vyāpāda*
3. Dullness and lethargy, *thīna-middha*
4. Doubt, *vicikicchā*
5. Restlessness and worry, *uddhacca-kukkucca*

Meditative development also means developing the five spiritual faculties, *indriya*:

1. Confidence, *saddhā*
2. Energy, *viriya*
3. Mindfulness, *sati*
4. Concentration, *samādhi*
5. Wisdom, *paññā*

Each hindrance obstructs one specific spiritual faculty: excitement of sensual pleasures obstructs confidence, ill will obstructs effort, dullness and lethargy obstruct mindfulness, doubt obstructs concentration, and restlessness and worry obstruct wisdom. Usually, restlessness and worry are considered the hindrances that obstruct concentration, but actually it is doubt that obstructs concentration.

To strengthen and develop the five spiritual faculties, we have to weaken and suppress the five hindrances: suppressing the excitement of sensual pleasures makes us calm, which increases our confidence; suppressing ill will also makes us calm and this increases our mental effort, our energy; suppressing dullness and lethargy increases mindfulness; suppressing doubt increases concentration; and finally, suppressing restlessness and worry increases our wisdom. By suppressing our hindrances, we strengthen and develop our spiritual faculties. This process is *bhāvanā*.

Why is concentration obstructed by doubt and not by restlessness and worry?

The Pali word for concentration is *samādhi*. We gain a degree of *samādhi* by methodically turning our attention to objects of meditation; this is the practice of *samatha-bhāvanā*. *Samādhi* gained in this way, however, is unstable and immediately breaks down as soon as some doubt arises. To stabilise and deepen *samādhi*, *samatha-bhāvanā* is practised in combination with *vipassanā-bhāvanā*. *Vipassanā* means insight, seeing things as they really are. By increasing our understanding of how things really are, we reduce our doubt and develop our confidence in the practice of meditation, in the spiritual way. Based on our own experiences, our confidence goes beyond mere views into the sphere of certainty.

When we are lacking in confidence about the practice of meditation, we are always thinking about things according to our cravings and do not see things as they really are. In the early stages of the practice, for example, we cling to traditional rites and rituals, offering this and that. Our confidence is still at the initial stage of merely views. If you attain to *sotāpanna*, you have destroyed your doubt about the spiritual way, and your *samādhi* may continue to develop. But to be completely free from restlessness and worry, you have to attain *arahatship*. This is why it is said that *samādhi* is obstructed by doubt.

In this world, there are many ways to relax: listen to music, take tranquillisers and drugs, drink alcohol, be hypnotised. People use countless different ways to relax and calm their minds. The main purpose of *bhāvanā*, however, is not to calm the mind; the main purpose is to understand the mind.

We use chalk to write on blackboards. When a piece of chalk drops to the floor and lands on its side, it breaks into two or three pieces. Similarly, when we use worldly ways to attain a sense of calm, our calm is fragile and can break at any time. Often, we are calm first thing in the morning but disturbed by the afternoon. Our minds are easily broken. When the piece of chalk lands on its end, it does not break; when we practise *bhāvanā* properly, our minds do not break.

On his daily walk, a man comes across a pile of rotting garbage. The garbage is lying right in the middle of his path; it looks and smells disgusting. Of course, the man wants to hide the garbage. He gets a shovel and covers the garbage with some soil. His path is now clear and he walks without being disturbed. A few days later a thunderstorm floods his path and washes away the soil—the garbage resurfaces.

"Oh," the man realises, "just hiding garbage isn't enough."

The man gets his shovel again. He digs into the pile and starts removing the garbage from his path. It is difficult work. He digs up bits of broken glass, barbed wire, rotting food, and many other dangerous and disgusting things. Even though faced with so much disgusting garbage, he continues to dig into the pile and remove the garbage until his path is completely clear. He now walks freely.

Trying to calm our minds through worldly ways just temporarily covers and hides the garbage on our paths. The garbage still lies below the surface. Even gaining *samādhi* through *samatha-bhāvanā*, we are just covering our garbage. We must dig out and remove the garbage. This is the *samādhi* gained through *vipassanā-bhāvanā*.

It is more important to see things as they really are than it is to attain a sense of calm. Calmness is not the most important thing in life. When we see things as they really are, when we understand the nature of reality through wisdom, we are not making any unwanted problems for ourselves. We live a peaceful life and *samādhi* naturally arises. Seeing things as they really are is the purpose of meditative development. If we want a peaceful life, we have to meditate.

How do I meditate?

It is difficult to explain how to meditate in just a few words, but I will explain a little.

A tightrope walker has to pay very keen attention to his mental and physical actions while walking on the rope. He is not looking to the right, to the left, ahead, or behind. He is not thinking about what will happen after walking on the rope and not thinking about what happened before. He cannot walk too slowly and he cannot walk too quickly; he must walk at just the right speed. And he is not thinking it is a good or bad thing to walk on the rope, nor is he making a lot of wishes for his future. The tightrope walker is only paying attention to where he is placing his foot on the rope, and he walks straight ahead.

To progress on our path, we also must try to avoid attending to mental and physical actions that take us away from the wholesome, take us away from seeing things as they really are. Arising in linked pairs, eight actions take us away:

- Coveting and grieving, *abhijjhā* and *domanassa*
- Having cravings and harnessing cravings, *icchā* and *kappana*
- Thinking about the future and thinking about the past, *anāgata* and *atīta*
- Doing things too quickly and doing things too slowly, *sīghaṃ* and *manda*

When we engage in one of these eight actions, we are not paying attention to what is actually happening in the present. We are not meditating and have walked off the path. On the other hand, when we do manage to remove ourselves from these eight mental and physical actions, our attention is wholesome and we see things as they really are. We stay in the middle of the path. We do not look to either side, we do not walk too slowly, and we do not walk too quickly. When we get away from these eight actions, only wholesome attention remains; we have a good balance and—like the man on the tightrope—we easily walk the path. The Buddha gives an outline of the things to be developed and the things not to be developed in the Sevitabbāsevitabba Sutta of the Majjhima Nikāya.

For young trees to grow into strong and healthy adults it takes light, water, good soil, and many years. A strong and healthy meditation practice also takes the proper conditions and time to develop. But many people will not take the time. Impatient, they crave concentration; impatient, they hope for wisdom; impatient, they wish for something. People often have many expectations of meditation and when they fail to instantly realise their expectations, they get fed up, stop meditating, and do something else.

How to meditate is a difficult question to answer because there are many, many different methods of meditation. I can only give you a general idea. A meditator's method of meditation is dependent upon his or her character. There is not one universal method that works for everyone. For a teacher to give the correct method to the meditator, the teacher must first understand the meditator's unique character. Then and only then can a particular method be introduced and developed. There are some teachers who use only one fixed method of meditation for all their students. Some meditators benefit from the teacher's method but others will not. Nevertheless, some teachers still insist that their meditators use their particular method. This is not the proper way to teach meditation. The meditators who fail to benefit from the teacher's method lose interest in meditating and just stop.

What are the benefits of meditation?

There are several. The world in which we live contains a wide range of people. Many are busy as bees, while many are corrupt. When associating with busy people, meditation makes it possible for us to remain calm and patient, and when associating with corrupt people, meditation protects us from being corrupted. In a nutshell, meditation enables us to follow our own way. We can interact with anyone without conflict or disturbance. The world is restless, complex, and violent. If we meditate in this restless world, we will be peaceful; if we meditate in this complex world, we will live simply and easily; and if we meditate in this violent world, we will live a life of kindness and love. Meditation is not just about walking slowly. Meditation is a state of mind, our state of mind. It makes it possible to live a simple life without complexity and restlessness. Wherever we go, there is peace.

Meditation also frees us from the fear of death. King Mahānāma, a relative of the Buddha, was afraid of dying. He went to the Buddha for help.

"I was self-assured and confident," said Mahānāma, "when I left the palace today, but I came across a wild elephant raging through the city. I am the King. It was my duty to control this animal, but it came close to killing me. What will happen when I die?"

"There is no need to be afraid of your death," said the Buddha, "because you have strong confidence in the Triple Gem. For a long time now, you have practised generosity and, to a degree, self-discipline, *sīla*. If you continue to protect your precepts, you will have a good death."

With their future uncertain and all the world's religions asserting the existence of some form of hell, many people are afraid to die. But if they meditate honestly, their fear of being born in a hell will disappear.

Arising out of our ignorance about the nature of reality, we are burdened with countless fears. To alleviate our fears, we cling to religions and philosophies that offer explanations. When we embrace a system of views, we feel a little more secure.

Meditation is not a system of views, is not dogma, not a philosophy, nor a religion. There is only the ongoing freethinking process. When we are meditating, we are not clinging to any philosophy or any religion. Yes, the meditator is religious, but he or she does not cling to one particular religion. The meditator is free from views, not thinking: "I am this" or "I am that." Instead, the meditator has kindness, compassion, and wisdom. The mind is free. These are the benefits of meditation.

What do I need before I can practise meditation?

You need a clear and free mind—clear and free of expectations. Usually, people have many expectations of meditation. They want to gain concentration, gain *jhānas*, or escape a problem. For instance, getting a divorce is a common problem.

I know!

Property, a job, a spouse, or a child—something has been lost. The person is now depressed and in emotional difficulty, and wants to escape. Everyone has problems. We first have to listen to peoples' problems before we can tell them about meditation. Before anything else, people need to be consoled. I do not advise anyone to gain concentration. No. When people are ready, I only suggest they try to see the reality of this world and the reality of their own minds. If people are willing to honestly look at their own minds, they will progress in meditation quite fast.

I said earlier that the *samādhi* gained through *vipassanā-bhāvanā* is more stable than the *samādhi* gained solely through *samatha-bhāvanā*. *Vipassanā* is also more beneficial to us than merely *samatha* because *vipassanā* destroys our ignorance and delusion. *Sati* and wisdom are *vipassanā-bhāvanā*'s base; they never get mixed up with delusion and ignorance.

In the early morning, pure dewdrops capture and reflect the rays of the sun. In contrast, muddy dewdrops do not. Even though the sun shines, muddy dewdrops never capture the rays of the sun. The sun is *nibbāna*, pure dewdrops are minds free of ignorance and delusion, and muddy dewdrops are minds defiled with ignorance and delusion. When our minds are free of ignorance, we capture the light of *nibbāna*. We reflect a purity that is like *nibbāna*. When, however, our minds are mixed up with ignorance and delusion, we do not. We will never understand *nibbāna* until we are like that pure dewdrop. We need to free ourselves from defilements; we need to free ourselves from ignorance.

We have to be very clear on this point: we want to destroy the ignorance of our minds. And it is through understanding and seeing the reality of this world that we travel towards calmness, tranquillity, and *nibbāna*. For example, meditators at the beginning of their journey ought to be able to perceive the beauty in nature without prejudice, without clinging to the beauty in nature. Many meditators, however, have strongly conditioned minds and are unable to get away from prejudice and clinging. Instead of travelling the path towards *nibbāna*, they travel another path. We have to see the flowing of all objects as they really are. To a certain extent, the meditator should have that ability from the beginning: be free of clinging to anything, just observe.

If you ask people what they are doing with their lives, you will get many different answers: we are eating, we are working, we are sleeping, etc. But there are three things that we all do. The first is breathing. It is very natural to breathe. We need not think, oh, I want to breathe. Breathing happens automatically. The second is thinking. We are also always thinking. Wherever we go, the thinking process is there. And the third is ageing. We need not think about ageing either. It happens. We are getting older. Breathing, thinking, and ageing—these three are common to all of us.

Wherever we go and whatever we do, these three are always with us and always happening. They have been happening from the time we were born and will continue until our deaths. They happen automatically. No matter where we go to meditate—Myanmar or Thailand or maybe England—these three are still with us. There may be minor differences between the objects of one country and another, but these differences are only external. When we travel to these places, our minds travel with us. Our minds do not change just because we change countries.

Meditation is not about switching anything off just because it is happening. Meditation is about understanding what is happening. We are trying to understand breathing, thinking, and aging; we are trying to understand our bodies; and we are trying to understand our minds. Within our own bodies of one or two metres and fifty kilos or more, we come to understand what is really happening. There is no need to go beyond these two metres, although if a person is just beginning to learn about meditation, a quiet place may be helpful. Still, even beginners need only one or two weeks in a quiet place.

If a person is spending many years trying to get away from sounds and noises, there is something wrong with their mind. Isolating ourselves from sounds and noises only leads to anger and conflicts when we are confronted with sounds and noises. After the Buddha became enlightened, he spent most of his life close to busy and noisy cities. If you read the suttas, you will find that only occasionally did he go to the forest and ask that no one come to visit. Except for the person who brought food, he was alone for maybe a month, but he always returned to the city.

The practice of *bhāvanā* is not about switching anything off. It is about understanding, it is about reducing our hindrances, and it is about developing our spiritual faculties. You have everything you need to practise *bhāvanā*.

"With sensual passion I burn. My mind is on fire.
Please, Gotama, from compassion, tell me how to put it out."

Venerable Vangisa—Ānanda Sutta[3]

2 Discipline

PEMASIRI THERA: Discipline is the foundation for meditative development. At the start of the *saṅgha*, the Buddha's first students were Brahmins and royalty who had a high moral standard. These people knew how to conduct themselves appropriately and he did not have to lay down any disciplinary rules of conduct for them. But later on many people, from a wide range of backgrounds, entered the *saṅgha* and many of these people did not know what was appropriate or what was inappropriate. Consequently, the Buddha began laying down a code of discipline to guide as well as to control the *bhikkhus*, the novices, and the laity. The Buddha had to teach these people how to share duties and live in harmony with others.

Every day, Buddhist laity try to follow five precepts of self-discipline, abstaining from: (1) killing, (2) stealing, (3) sensual misconduct, (4) lying, and (5) the use of intoxicants. On *Poya* days, when laity go to the temple to practise meditation, they follow three more precepts, abstaining from: (6) eating after midday, (7) dancing, singing, music, shows, as well as wearing garlands, scents, cosmetics, and jewellery, and (8) sleeping on luxurious beds. *Bhikkhus* follow ten precepts. In addition to the laity's first five, they follow an additional five, abstain from: (6) eating after midday, (7) dancing, singing, music, and shows, (8) wearing garlands, scents, cosmetics and jewellery, (9) sleeping on luxurious beds, and (10) accepting gold and silver. The *bhikkhus*' seventh and eighth precepts form the laity's seventh precept, while the *bhikkhus*' ninth precept is the laity's eighth.

Before the time of the Buddha, people in India practised these same five, eight, and ten precepts; the Buddha was not the first person in history to recommend them. The precepts, even the eight and ten precepts, already existed in Indian culture. What the Buddha did lay down for the first time were the two hundred and twenty-seven rules of discipline for *bhikkhus*.

In the Sekha Sutta of the Majjhima Nikāya, Venerable Ānanda speaks to the Sakyans of Kapilavatthu of the discipline in higher training.

Self-discipline, *sīla*, has two aspects:

1. Abstaining from inappropriate conduct, *vāritta-sīla*
2. Engaging in appropriate conduct, *cāritta-sīla*

Abstaining from inappropriate conduct means following the precepts and society's basic rules. By abstaining, we support one another and conflicts are avoided. But just abstaining alone falls short. We must also actively engage in appropriate conduct, which means there is a commitment to the wholesome. Working out of compassion and loving-kindness, we support others and ourselves. In Buddhist terms, this means living according to the eightfold path. A reasonable way to live, the eightfold path spells out our responsibilities and the appropriateness of our actions. When we are responsible and act appropriately, that is all there is. Life is easy, simple, and not so difficult. For anyone living in any society, whether *bhikkhu* or lay, appropriate conduct is crucial.

Appropriate conduct is also the prerequisite for gaining meditative concentration of mind. It is obligatory. Concentration, *samādhi*, is easy to attain for people who conduct themselves appropriately. Many, if not most, meditators are unaware of just how important appropriate conduct is to the cultivation of *samādhi*. Bypassing conduct, meditators often try to gain concentration exclusively through control and suppression. For these meditators, meditative concentration means merely sitting in one posture for hours on end in a meditation hall. Many of these meditators get up from their sitting position only to take meals or go to the toilet, and will not do anything else. They just continually sit. Sometimes these meditators neglect to even wash themselves, but they will remain in the meditation hall and sit in one posture for hours and hours. That is not real *samādhi*. That is foolishness. There is no wisdom in this type of conduct and these meditators will fail to attain *samādhi* because they are conducting themselves inappropriately. They lack the essential foundation for *samādhi*.

The Buddha taught the practice of *āyati saṃvara sīla* to help people train in appropriate conduct and to help them restrain from indulging in inappropriate conduct. *Āyati* means to come close to, *saṃvara* means restraint, and *sīla* means discipline. The intention of this practice is to support taking on the work of discipline, *sīla*. Maintaining *sīla* requires wisdom and effort. The Buddha acknowledged that people, in exceptional circumstances or in the case of an accident, might occasionally conduct themselves inappropriately.

When *sīla* is broken, the practice of *āyati saṃvara sīla* enables people to cleanse themselves by immediately re-establishing their intention to keep *sīla*. If they again break *sīla*, through accident or whatever, they again establish their intention to keep *sīla* for the rest of their lives. This preserves their s*īla*. In this way they continue to train in appropriate conduct. The intention of *āyati saṃvara sīla* is to keep *sīla* for the rest of our lives. Keep it!

In our present-day society, however, many people use the teachings on *āyati saṃvara sīla* to excuse inappropriate conduct. Without being driven by exceptional circumstances or accident, many people intentionally conduct themselves inappropriately. For example, they get thoroughly intoxicated, acting and speaking badly. After knowingly indulging in inappropriate activities, they excuse their behaviour by using their view of *āyati saṃvara sīla* to theoretically cleanse themselves. After cleansing, they practise some restraint from inappropriate conduct in their daily lives, but later on intentionally indulge in inappropriate conduct. This type of behaviour has become a tradition: indulging in inappropriate conduct, cleansing, again temporarily practising restraint, and then again indulging. These people have no intention to keep *sīla* for the rest of their lives. Consequently, they never develop their mental qualities and they never make any progress in meditation.

The Pali word for abstinence is *virati*. Abstinence is far more important and beneficial to our meditative development than temporary restraint. Abstinence means we make as much effort as necessary to stop the performance of an unwholesome action. We make as much effort as necessary to stop our indulgence in inappropriate conduct. We stop breaking rules of discipline. Before we perform an unwholesome action by body or speech, we say no. We say to ourselves that we will refuse to indulge. We simply will not do it.

DAVID: Do we also abstain from unwholesome thoughts?

In the beginning, *sīla* only emphasises abstinence from inappropriate bodily actions and inappropriate speech. In the whole of the Buddha's code of discipline, the *vinaya*, there are no more than two rules that apply to the mind, and those two rules only apply to *bhikkhus* and do not apply to laity. To the lay people, the Buddha taught the restraining of thoughts only indirectly. He started their training at the basic level of restraining body and speech.

"There are these four types of people to be found existing in the world. Which four? One in darkness who is headed for darkness, one in darkness who is headed for light, one in light who is headed for darkness, and one in light who is headed for light."

The Buddha—Tamonata Sutta[4]

3 Concentration

PEMASIRI THERA: When you hear people arguing that this or that is *samādhi*, it is clear they don't have *samādhi*. What are your thoughts on the subject?

DAVID: *Samādhi* is sitting in concentration. My mind would be calm, not racing around.

STUDENT #2: I'd add there is a balancing of mind where investigation takes place.

Student #3: I recall what I was taught: the mind is pure; the hindrances are suppressed.

Yes, *samādhi* is generally translated as concentration of mind, and it is true that within *samādhi* there is a calmness, similar to the deep feeling of relief and relaxation at the end of the working day. But the calm that fills our bodies after work is not the real *samādhi* calm. It is also true the mind is not racing around and true there is a pureness, although you cannot say that a person in *samādhi* is just calmly sitting. Doing nothing but sitting for hours on end is not *samādhi*. No. *Samādhi* is different, as inside of *samādhi* is a sharp awareness. A person in *samādhi* is sharply aware of each and every object that arises in the mind. It may be a subtle object, but a person in *samādhi* is aware of the arising of that object.

One-pointedness of mind, *citt'ekaggatā*, is a term that is used to describe this sharp awareness. You see letters on pages in books. There is the letter A, the letter M, the letter D, and so on. There are hundreds of letters on a page and as you read you immediately recognise these letters. Your recognition of a letter means there is one-pointedness, unification, of your mind with the letter on the page. There is agreement between your mind and the letter. You focus in on the letter, there is only the letter in your mind at that time, and you recognise the letter. At once you recognise it. There is only that one object, the letter, in your mind at that exact moment in time. Our one-pointedness of mind catches and recognises various objects of perception. Without this characteristic of mind called *citt'ekaggatā*, we cannot apprehend any object.

Despite the fact that one-pointedness of mind, *citt'ekaggatā*, apprehends objects, it is a neutral factor that is present in the mental processes of all living beings. Every human being has it. Even animals have one-pointedness of mind. It is neither right nor wrong, neither wholesome nor unwholesome, neither skilful nor unskilful, and neither appropriate nor inappropriate. One-pointedness of mind simply alternates between objects of perception. It moves from apprehending one object to apprehending the next object, and then onto apprehending the next and so on. One-pointedness is the alternating point for mind. And though one-pointedness of mind is frequently used to define the sharp awareness of *samādhi*, it is actually only the starting point. It is not *samādhi*, but the starting point for *samādhi*. Nonetheless, one-pointedness does lead to *samādhi*.

There are many types of *samādhi*, concentration. It can be right and it can be wrong. Wrong *samādhi*, *micchā-samādhi*, we gain through clinging to objects that our senses find pleasurable: fine music, beautiful art, good tasting food, and so forth. Yes, this is a form of *samādhi*, but this is not right *samādhi* because there is attachment, clinging to these sensual pleasures. In contrast, right *samādhi*, *sammā-samādhi*, means there is no clinging. Right *samādhi* means the five hindrances are suppressed and the true nature of the object is seen.

The true nature of objects is impermanency, unsatisfactoriness, and insubstantiality: *anicca*, *dukkha*, and *anatta*. When *samādhi* is properly developed, we clearly see these three characteristics in each and every object we contact with our senses. We hear a sound. When we contact the sound with right *samādhi*, with right concentration, we perceive the true nature of it. We perceive the sound's impermanency, the sound's unsatisfactoriness, and the sound's insubstantiality— *anicca*, *dukkha*, and *anatta*. Right *samādhi* enables us to recognise these three characteristics in the sound. When we clearly perceive the true nature of the sound, we do not experience sadness, fear, or anger towards it. There is only some intention to let go of that sound. We do not choose to be entertained by the sound and instead turn to investigation.

There is no wisdom in just repeating over and over that the objects we contact in the world are impermanent, unsatisfactory, and insubstantial. No wisdom at all in just repeating that these three characteristics of existence—*anicca*, *dukkha*, and *anatta*—are the reality of every object we contact. *Anicca*, *dukkha*, and *anatta* are just words, words that can be repeated by anyone of any philosophy or religion. We must come to know the three characteristics of existence through a properly developed *samādhi*, through the experience of proper concentration.

Properly developed *samādhi* is the four fine-material mental absorptions, the four *rūpa-jjhānas*:

- The first fine-material mental absorption, *paṭhamajjhāna*
- The second fine-material mental absorption, *dutiyajjhāna*
- The third fine-material mental absorption, *tatiyajjhāna*
- The fourth fine-material mental absorption, *catutthajjhāna*

Jhāna is an alert, lucid, and non-deluded state of consciousness.

When *samādhi* is properly developed, we perceive the true nature of the objects we contact with our senses. Wherever we go, no matter which objects we contact, we know these objects are impermanent, unsatisfactory, and without any self or substance. And as a result, we have fewer problems. When *samādhi* is not properly developed, we never see these three characteristics of existence. As a result of failing to perceive the reality of objects, we have many problems.

Sīla, the first division of the eightfold path, is the foundation for developing *samādhi*. Conducting ourselves appropriately, we are careful of everything we say and do. We speak words that are true, kind, and beneficial. From the simplest of actions, we act with good intention and generosity. We allow others to live in peace. These are very basic things. By practising *sīla* we clean up our mental environment, clean inside, and settle our minds.

Many people appear to be practising appropriate conduct. Yes, they seem to be living according to *sīla*, but their minds are disturbed because they overindulge in sensual pleasures, *kāma-cchanda*. They are constantly trying to fulfil their cravings for sensual pleasures, and, if such people continue to live in this way, they will never properly develop their *samādhi*. I am not saying we gain *samādhi* simply by practising strict self-control. Meditators that blindly follow many rules without an understanding of why they are following rules are simply torturing themselves, *atta-kilamatha*. And the *samādhi* they gain through such wilful self-dominance is not the real *samādhi*; they are just beating themselves up. *Samādhi* does not come through blind adherence to many rules nor does it come through excessive self-control.

Samādhi arises out of wisdom. When meditators have some understanding of what they are doing and understand why they practise *sīla*, they sensibly avoid overindulging in sensual pleasures and avoid torturing themselves. When we settle down our minds in both these ways, concentration is not so difficult to gain. Even in city meditation centres, we can properly develop our *samādhi* and attain *jhāna*.

David: I thought a forest hermitage was needed to attain *jhāna*.

No. We need not go to the forest to develop *samādhi*, to just attain *jhāna*. After having attained *jhāna*, we go to the forest in order to train the mind to remain in *jhāna* for longer periods of time, to strengthen the *samādhi*.

For effective training, four types of support are necessary:

1. People, *puggala*
2. Food, *āhāra*
3. Lodging, *senāsana*
4. Climate, *utu*

The people must be supportive, food needs to be nutritious, lodging has to meet basic requirements, and the climate ought to agree with us. Some prefer to live in the cool while others prefer the warm. These four supports are necessary for training the mind in *samādhi*.

People are our prime support. We must associate with people who are compatible, create few problems in our community, practise *sīla*, and share the same goals. Friends. When we live on a daily basis with good friends, we maintain the practice and progress.

At this moment, there are six of us in our meditation group. Each of us has his or her own attitudes, ideas, and opinions. Each of us has his or her own way of doing things. To support each other, we occasionally surrender our individual ways and yield to another person's way. Right? We have to let go of always doing what we want to do.

This principle is illustrated in the Cūḷagosiṅga Sutta of the Majjhima Nikāya. Three *arahats* live together in the park of the Gosinga Sāla-tree Wood and one evening the Buddha visits them. "We are different in body," they say to the Buddha, "but one in mind."[5]

People sometimes forget such crucial things, forget to be civilised, and consequently there is no gaining of *samādhi*. They are unsupportive. They engage in disruptive speech: do this; do that; do not do this; you are impossible; you must stop making so much noise. When it is quiet, someone else says there is no need to be so quiet; we must be relaxed. And they begin making noise. These people are forgetting to support each other and it is better to live alone than it is to live with them. When you live alone, you will have your own way, and, if you really need *samādhi*, you will be able to develop your *samādhi* and use it. Certainly, it is better to have two or three understanding and supportive friends with you than it is to live alone. But if you cannot find supportive friends, living alone is the best option.

When everyone in a meditation centre—*bhikkhus* as well as laity—works together with the same effort and mindfulness, the centre functions as it should and calm naturally arises. We actually learn *bhāvanā*, even bring the practice up to a high level and get into it properly when all of us work together, in harmony. When the bell rings in the morning, we start the day. We all start the day at the appropriate time, not just when we feel like starting the day.

Nonetheless, for a couple of reasons, it is difficult for meditators in the average city centre to go beyond a preliminary level of *samādhi* and progress through the *jhānas*. First, not all *bhikkhus* and laity in city centres support the meditator's practice. I am not saying that *bhikkhus* in city centres do not have *sīla*. Most *bhikkhus* do have *sīla*. But because *bhikkhus* and laity choose to engage themselves in a variety of activities besides *jhāna*—teaching, counselling, writing, providing services to the community—the meditator's practice gets disrupted. To go beyond a preliminary level of *samādhi*, meditators must be able to maintain their practice without disruption for a long period of time.

Secondly, teachers and their meditators need privacy. If someone happens to come by while the teacher is discussing personal aspects of the practice with the meditator, they immediately stop their discussion. When I speak with a meditator about his or her practice, a third person generally isn't present unless I am instructing a foreigner in which case a translator sits in. When I discuss meditation in Sinhalese—with old, young, or middle-aged—no one else sits in. In busy centers, people are always walking in on meditation discussions; thus, the meditator's practice can only be taught up to a preliminary level. In ancient Sri Lankan hermitages, *bhikkhus* discussed the practice in a private hall, a *dham sabha mandapaya*.

For the meditator to maintain his or her mind in *samādhi* for longer periods of time, they need to go to a forest hermitage. When I was young, I travelled around Sri Lanka and visited several hermitages. At the good hermitages, each day began with one *bhikkhu* cleaning the dining hall before he and all the other *bhikkhus* went for alms. The first *bhikkhu* to return prepared the hall, setting out the drinking and washing water for the others. As the other *bhikkhus* returned from alms, they ate their meals in the hall, cleaned up after themselves, and then retired to their *kuṭis*. All the *bhikkhus* did this. The last *bhikkhu* to return from alms did one final cleaning of the hall. These *bhikkhus* never waited for someone else to do work that had to be done; they simply did whatever work was required. Everyone worked together.

Over the course of about twelve years, I lived in a variety of places, such as Arankele. I also once lived in a forest near the Potuvil area that was infested with elephants. The area is now under the control of the LTTE. As part of the meditation training, I never went home to visit my family; only my teacher and mother knew my whereabouts. At times, I was fortunate to share the company of Bhante Vimalo of Kelaniya. With him in his thirties and me in my twenties, he gave me a lot of support. I did not go to the forest to experience hardship. No. I went to the forest in order to train in these practices.

Are you still doing these practices?

No. I have not done this type of meditation for a long time. And since I do not have these *jhānas* any more, I find it difficult to remember what my state of mind was like when I was living in the forest and training in these practices. To remember back to that time in my life, I need a peaceful state of mind.

Through studying and reading books, we can gain a great deal of knowledge about *samādhi* and the *jhānas*. But book knowledge alone is not sufficient to properly discuss this topic. We are talking about training in specific meditation practices. The experiences must be there. When the teacher has firsthand experience in *samādhi*, he or she can teach it. When the student has firsthand experience he or she can discuss it.

"From inappropriate attention, you're being chewed up by your thoughts. Relinquishing what's inappropriate, contemplate appropriately."

A deva—Yoniso Manasikāra Sutta[6]

4 Wisdom

DAVID: Yesterday, a person told me Buddhism is foolish, and what the Buddha taught 2,500 years ago is now irrelevant.

PEMASIRI THERA: The Buddha's words are still relevant. He recommended keeping company with wise people and avoiding fools.

I feel working in a tsunami camp is more useful than meditating.

It is good to help people, but there is a limit to what one person can do for any other person. *Kamma* is complicated. Being rich, poor, or anything in between is no guarantee of either happiness or misery. Quite the contrary. Many rich people are miserable while many poor people are very happy. There is no correlation between wealth and happiness. The most valuable thing you will ever learn or ever help anyone else to find is wisdom. Wisdom is the greatest gift because it ends suffering.

Three Foundations of Wisdom

Wisdom, *paññā* in Pali, rests on three foundations:

1. Knowledge, *ñāṇa*
2. Understanding, *avabodha*
3. Realisation by oneself, *paccattaṃ veditabba*

Through studying with teachers, reading books, and talking with friends, we come to understand a great deal about a great many things. Practical, worldly knowledge helps us to progress through our daily lives. People use knowledge to become scientists, engineers, and doctors. Because an engineer has knowledge of structures, he can assess a building's faults and make improvements. And because a doctor has a good knowledge of the body, she can diagnose a patient's disease and prescribe remedies. Knowledge is very useful in this world, in this *lokiya*.

What do we mean by *lokiya*?

I think *lokiya* means our mundane world. It is a place filled with people, animals, trees, mountains, rivers, and life. Many things. *Saṃsāra*.

Hondai! Good answer. What is *saṃsāra*?

The cycle of taking a birth, living, old age, sickness, death, and again another birth. *Saṃsāra* also means I am making the same things, like mistakes, over and over again.

Who will be born again?

Me. I'll be born again.

Who?

I don't know who or what.

The person called I is born again. The person called I creates everything and thus owns everything. You will find the person called I from our human world in the sense-sphere realm right through to the fine-material and immaterial realms. All three realms are of the mundane sphere of existence, *lokiya*.[7]

The development of knowledge supports seeing the reality of these three realms. By investigating the nature of phenomena in the sense-sphere realm, scientists determine the properties of materiality, *rūpa*. And by investigating the nature of phenomena in the fine-material and immaterial realms, meditators determine the nature of mentality, *nāma*. In addition to discovering physical realities of the sense-sphere realm, meditators study their minds.

Knowledge dictates abilities. Using their knowledge of materiality, engineers design telephones that send information around the world and chemists formulate fertilisers that nurture crops. Using knowledge of materiality as well as mentality—the immaterial—doctors treat physical and mental illnesses. Knowledge of materiality and immateriality is very useful in this world. Meditators use their knowledge of immateriality to perform mental feats. With their mind developed to *jhāna*, a meditator has the psychic ability to send information anywhere in the world; a telephone is not necessary. And by just using mind, the meditator can materialise elements; this ability is called *iddhividha*. The chemist makes water by physically combining hydrogen and oxygen; the meditator makes water by using mind. Both Christ and Buddha had supernormal abilities. Christ was powerful: he replicated food and made it rain.

During the Buddha's time, many people had developed their mental abilities to a high degree. Gᵛnana was an Indian woman who replicated herself. Others bent metal with their minds.

Engineers, chemists, doctors, and strong meditators—all have developed their unique knowledge to high levels and they are putting it to good use. When, however, our goal is to overcome our own personal suffering, it is more important to develop meditative knowledge than it is to develop worldly knowledge. We use the knowledge we gain through the practice of meditation to see things as they really are and attain liberation from *saṃsāra*. This is fundamental. Some scientists have extremely high levels of knowledge, yet are afraid of their spouses.

With the exception of *buddhas*, *pacceka-buddhas*, and *arahats*, everyone is disturbed by eight worldly conditions that are named in the Saṅgīti Sutta of the Dīgha Nikāya:

- Profit and loss
- Fame and shame
- Praise and blame
- Pleasure and pain

To overcome these disturbances, good meditators develop their knowledge of the nature of reality. With some kindness and some understanding of the law of *kamma*, they gain *jhāna* and become good people. Clearly seeing in the sense-sphere, fine-material, and immaterial realms, good people help others and themselves. If they choose, they can even influence bad people.

Like the early teachers of the Buddha, after good people die they tend to take birth in the higher planes of existence of the immaterial realm. In contrast, a bad person tends towards birth in the lower planes of the sense-sphere realm. Nonetheless, a good person is still worldly and can be influenced by a bad person, which means a good person can potentially take birth in one of the lower planes, such as the animal. Because a good person is still not a very good person, they can go upwards or downwards after their deaths.

To be very good, people must attain a supramundane plane of liberation, *lokuttara*.[8] Having realised the path and fruit of the supramundane, very good people are faultless and noble. And though attracting both good and bad people, neither the good nor the bad can influence or disturb them. Very good people always take birth in the higher planes of existence and never in the lower. Roughly, one in ten is a good person and one in a thousand is a very good person.

The sense-sphere, fine-material, and immaterial realms are all still within *saṃsāra*'s cycle of birth and death, and therefore unsatisfactory. To escape *saṃsāra*, to escape these mundane realms, we use meditative knowledge to attain the supramundane planes of liberation. Knowledge supports this development in wisdom.

Knowledge, however, is not wisdom. Whereas the same knowledge can belong to many different people, wisdom cannot possibly belong to another. Being experiential, wisdom belongs completely to you. It is something that is gained through personal realisation, *paccattaṃ veditabba*. It comes through from you.

Why do we need wisdom?

We need wisdom for many things. We need it to see and understand the process of cause and effect. When causes and effects are clearly seen, we see a release from those causes and effects. We also need wisdom to see the three characteristics of existence: *anicca*, *dukkha*, and *anatta*. We need wisdom to understand *saṃsāra*, to know which path to walk, and finally, to break free of this *saṃsāric* realm and realise the happiness of *nibbāna*. *Nibbāna* is independent of the mundane realms of existence, the *lokiya*. We need wisdom to fully understand the mundane realms and attain realisation.

By making better use of his or her mind's potential than, say, the worldly scientist, a *sotāpanna* penetrates the true nature of existence and attains path; he or she realises the first plane of liberation from the mundane. Using about 40% of his or her mind's potential, an *arahat* attains enlightenment. Venerables Sāriputta and Mogallāna used in the region of 60% of their minds' potential, and the Buddha used his mind to its maximum.

Does seeing the three characteristics of existence mean I am increasing my wisdom?

Yes. At the beginning of the practice, we have a limited understanding into the true nature of existence: we see *anicca*, *dukkha*, and *anatta* but only vaguely. By meditating, our understanding of the world develops and our wisdom likewise develops. Anyone who sees the three characteristics very clearly—attains realisation into the true nature of the world—really has wisdom.

Without wisdom, we misunderstand what the Buddha meant by the term *anicca*, impermanence. We see cars rusting, buildings decaying, plants withering, our friends dying and we think this is what he meant. Though happening because of *anicca*, the wear and tear on physical things that we see with our naked eyes is only the gross change, *vipariṇāma*, that all conditioned things undergo. Gross change is common knowledge. We all know that cars rust, buildings decay, and people die.

When the Buddha talked about *anicca*, he meant something far more profound and subtle than gross change. *Anicca* is the change that all conditioned phenomena undergo on a moment-to-moment basis; it is microscopic change. Whether things are physical or mental, they have the characteristic of undergoing change every moment. They arise and pass away, continually. Whatever comes into being is subject to decay and death—every moment. We generally don't see *anicca*. But if we watch carefully, *anicca* can be seen.

I have drawn a red line on this whiteboard. We normally just see the line on the board and fail to see *anicca*. While the line is being drawn, changes are continually happening. Right from the time I began to draw the line all the way through until the time I finished, there were changes to be seen. Before I began to draw, this was a blank whiteboard. As I draw the line, part of the whiteboard changes to red. That is impermanence, *anicca*. The pen's ink is being used up, my hand is moving, and I am thinking. All of these things are also *anicca*. From the time we started this discussion right up until this present moment, we only see *anicca*. There is nothing else to be seen but *anicca*. Everything is impermanent, always changing.

We try, however, to keep our world stable, without anything ever changing. You, for example, are tape-recording these talks and sometimes I have to cough. The microphone picks up the sound of my cough and I feel this is bad because I do not accept *anicca*. And just now, one man disturbed us by slamming a door and another by talking nearby. That is also *anicca*. We take these impermanent objects as permanent and we suffer.

"Why," we wonder, "do these men forget to support the learning of *dhamma*? Why are they behaving so badly?" I am suffering because I am failing to see impermanence. I am only seeing gross change.

Ariya-kosalla is the knowledge as well as the understanding of how to live in the present moment. We use *ariya-kosalla* to adjust to conditions in order to make progress. We need it to live in this world. We learn many different things in life. But all of what we learn is of little use if we fall short of learning how to live in this present moment. The man who just now slammed the door with a loud bang and disturbed our talk is unaware of how to live in the present moment. He has neither knowledge nor understanding of what we are doing here, and this is why he behaved so badly. Having no *cāritta sīla*, no manners, it is difficult for him to understand the three characteristics of existence. To progress on the path, we all need to know how to adjust to the present moment. We must include *ariya-kosalla* in our practice. When we walk, we sometimes come across places where a staircase would be useful, but there is no staircase. If we want to take a step forward, we have to adjust our way of doing things. Looking around and finding a ladder, we climb it and go forward.

When Prince Siddhārtha came upon an old man, he asked himself: "Why did this man become old? Why did he change? And why does everyone have to become old and die?" Having seen change, Prince Siddhārtha then set out to discover the causes for change. In due course, he discovered the three characteristics of existence: *anicca*, *dukkha,* and *anatta*.

We live in the human world of the mundane realms of existence, *lokiya*. It is impossible to keep things in our world stable, without change. All things in our world are subject to *anicca*. *Anicca*, *dukkha*, and *anatta*—these three characteristics of existence must be in the back of our minds at all times. If we really understand what is *anicca*, there is no I. If we attain realisation, *paccattaṃ veditabba*, there is only *anatta*. When we talk about the three characteristics of existence, we are talking about wisdom, *paññā*.

Three Types of Wisdom

There are three types of wisdom:

1. Wisdom based-on-learning, *sutamaya-paññā*
2. Wisdom based-on-thinking: *cintāmaya-paññā*
3. Wisdom based-on-mental-development, *bhāvanāmaya-paññā*

We call them types of wisdom, *paññā*, because they help us to attain *nibbāna*. They are the highest, ultimate conditions, *paramattha-paccaya*.

Wisdom based-on-learning, *sutamaya-paññā*, is *paññā* acquired through the process of listening to others. We hear, learn, and acquire some wisdom. Wisdom based-on-learning has a theoretical basis. The Pali word *suta* means heard. In the context of *sutamaya-paññā*, *suta* specifically refers to hearing words from religious authorities, such as the Buddha. People heard the word of the Buddha and learned. The Buddha inspired them. This is why suttas begin with the Pali expression *evaṃ me sutaṃ*, which means: "Thus have I heard." Unlike today, many people in the time of the Buddha learned through hearing just a few words.

The second type of *paññā* is wisdom based-on-thinking, *cintāmaya-paññā*. It is wisdom we acquire through our own thinking, without learning from others. Wisdom based-on-thinking means we reflect on a subject. We wonder if this or that is right or wrong. We ask ourselves: "What is the true nature of this and that?" We investigate. For example, by reflecting on what we hear in our *dhamma* discussions, we learn from them. You might wonder if what I am saying is correct. You investigate what I say and eventually come to some personal understanding. It is through wisdom based-on-thinking that we come to know the nature of contact, feeling, perception, and volition. Reflecting on these mental factors, we come to a clear understanding of them. By continually thinking about the mental factors, we increase our knowledge and understanding of them. By reflecting and investigating, we are developing our wisdom based-on-thinking; we are developing our *paññā*. Small streams come together and make a big stream, a river.

The third type of *paññā* is wisdom based-on-mental-development, *bhāvanāmaya-paññā*. *Bhāvanā* has two meanings: reduce the five hindrances, *nīvaraṇa*, and develop the five spiritual faculties, *indriya*. Excitement of sensual pleasures, ill will, dullness and lethargy, doubt, and restlessness and worry—these we have to reduce. Confidence, mental effort, mindfulness, concentration, and wisdom—all of these we have to develop.

Since the five hindrances obstruct our five spiritual faculties, we develop the latter by reducing the former. When we reduce our first hindrance of excitement of sensual pleasures, the mind becomes calm and clear and quiet, and this develops our confidence. Reducing our ill will also results in a calm and clear mind; this develops our mental effort, our energy. Reducing dullness and lethargy develops our mindfulness. The fourth hindrance is usually listed as restlessness and worry, but it is by reducing our doubt that we develop our concentration. Doubt is actually our fourth hindrance. And finally, by reducing our restlessness and worry, we develop our wisdom, our *paññā*. We have to reduce, temporarily suppress, these five hindrances to develop the five spiritual faculties; this is *bhāvanā*. Wisdom based-on-mental-development, *bhāvanāmaya-paññā*, is the understanding and realisation we gain through this process of reducing our hindrances and developing our spiritual faculties.

Just how important is a good teacher?

A teacher is essential. Students obtain wisdom based-on-learning when their teacher says something that is relevant to their lives. This has nothing to do with the questions the students ask of their teacher. No. Wisdom based-on-learning means an understanding arises in the minds of the students; the students approach the words of the teacher. The ultimate instance of wisdom based-on-learning is the student who attains path knowledge as soon as he or she hears the right words from their teacher. The teachings worked to their maximum. In the Buddha's time, many people attained path knowledge from just a few of his inspirational words. Now, such people are rarely found.

Suṇātha manasikarotha bhāsissāmi. Said at the beginning of *dhamma* talks, this Pali expression means: "Please listen and reflect; I will speak. Listen carefully to what I am saying and consider what I am saying." Just now, you asked a question. I could say: "*Suṇātha manasikarotha bhāsissāmi*." Please pay attention to what I have to say. Listen carefully. Listen well. I will answer your question.

Suṇātha means you direct your ears towards me. *Manasikarotha* means you closely follow the words I am saying. Your mind is going along with what I say and your mind changes upon hearing the words spoken. You are not just sitting there, with my words going in one ear and out the other. No. Your mind is always going along the way it is being led.

The Buddha said that listening to the *dhamma* has five benefits:

1. Hearing new ideas
2. Clarifying old ideas
3. Uplifting the mind
4. Reducing and destroying doubts
5. Straightening out one's view

These benefits come to us through wisdom based-on-learning. Wisdom based-on-learning is important. It supports the development of wisdom based-on-thinking and also supports wisdom based-on-mental-development.

The majority of people who attained path and fruit in the Buddha's time attained them through wisdom based-on-learning; after hearing the *dhamma*, they attained. *Buddhas* and *pacceka-buddhas* independently attain path and fruit through wisdom based-on-thinking; they think things through and attain. And lastly, wisdom based-on-mental-development, *bhāvanā*, is us.

I don't understand.

People like us. The wisdom we acquire through learning supports our acquiring wisdom through thinking and *bhāvanā*. Learning enables us to reflect on the nature of reality and this supports attaining the experiential. This is the way the three types of *paññā* grow.

Remember that understanding is the second foundation of *paññā* and we make understanding arise through the development of our wisdom based-on-thinking, *cintāmaya-paññā*. *Cintā* means thinking and reflecting, which requires developing five factors of knowledge, *ñāṇa*:

1. Applied thought, *vitakka*
2. Sustained thought, *vicāra*
3. Mental effort, energy, *viriya*
4. Mental attention, *manasikāra*
5. One-pointedness of mind, *citt'ekaggatā*

When these five factors are well developed and well directed, understanding arises. To gain an understanding in *dhamma*, these factors of knowledge have to be in operation. Great scientists, such as Einstein, develop these five factors to a high level.

Does wisdom based-on-thinking mean we argue with ourselves?

Argue is the wrong word to use for developing wisdom based-on-thinking. You debate and reflect on points until you attain the highest level, until you see that existence is a process of mental and material phenomena continually arising. We develop knowledge and understanding, and eventually attain realisation.

The first type of *paññā* is wisdom based-on-learning. It is theoretical knowledge we hear from others. The second type of *paññā* is wisdom based-on-thinking. It is the intellectual wisdom we gain through our own reflections. And the third type of *paññā* is wisdom based-on-mental-development, which is the genuine understanding—the realisation—we gain through meditation.

Of the three types of *paññā*, wisdom based-on-learning and wisdom based-on-thinking help more in worldly affairs than does wisdom based-on-mental-development, although wisdom based-on-mental-development does also help to some extent in the world. *Samatha* meditation practices are actually worldly practices. They help people remain calm and patient in their worldly activities, in the mundane realm. The *dhamma* we are discussing, however, is separate from living a worldly life.

Our normal understanding of the nature of existence, such as the understanding required to be a scientist, is like a banana plant. A banana plant produces one bunch of bananas and then dies. A new stalk then grows from the rhizome, from the old roots of the original banana plant. The new stalk is a regeneration of the same banana plant. Similarly, our normal understanding of existence leads to endless rounds of taking birth, *saṃsāra*.

Functioning differently from our normal understanding, *paññā* is more like the palmyra palm tree. Palmyras are flowering plants that use seeds to reproduce. When a palmyra dies, no new stalk grows from its root. The original palmyra is completely wiped out when it dies and will not sprout up again. That is the last stage for the original palmyra. If we have *paññā*, we see the three characteristics, gain freedom from this *saṃsāric* realm, and go directly to *nibbāna*. Like a palmyra palm tree, we never take birth again.

You have seen people burning small pieces of camphor near the Bodhi Tree. They look like flakes of wax. When you burn oil, there is some residue. But when you burn a piece of camphor, there is no residue whatsoever. The whole piece of camphor burns out and nothing remains of it. The same is possible for us. We use *paññā* to see the three characteristics in every object, burn the whole of *saṃsāra*, and attain *nibbāna*. When we understand everything through *paññā*, nothing remains in our stores. When we burn even just a small section of one piece of camphor, the small section we burn is completely destroyed and leaves no residue. Similarly, when we manage to burn even just a small piece of *saṃsāra*—attain some realisation into *saṃsāra*'s nature through *paññā*—that amount of *saṃsāra* is destroyed and will never come again. When you attain to *sotāpanna*, there is no birth in hell or in any other lower world. That is definite.

Paññā has completely destroyed the possibility of going down to a lower birth. When you become an *anāgāmī*, you will never come back to this sense-sphere realm. The possibility of returning here is completely destroyed. When you become an *arahat*, everything is destroyed. There is nothing to come back to anywhere. There is nothing to be reborn. These are the things done by *paññā*.

What you are saying is different from what is said by some other schools of Buddhism. Some say a person can attain high stages of liberation and then backslide to a lower stage.

All the world's religious traditions say we have to return to somewhere. This is why we have to see things through *paññā*, have to see everything clearly, and have to let go of such views. When we make a mental note, it needs to be through *paññā*. We are not trying to push things away, to switch anything off. No. We are just trying to see clearly, see the true nature of existence, and see reality. When we see the world through *paññā*, the defilements do not arise. When we see everything through *paññā*, we attain extinction of suffering, *nirodha*.

Nirodha is different from losing something. If we lose something, we can find it again. What we lose can reappear. *Nirodha* is different. Nothing ever arises from *nirodha*. There is nothing in *nirodha* to give birth and there is nothing to be found in *nirodha* that we can take. *Nirodha* is purely an extinction of suffering. To attain *nirodha*, we have to train our minds to stop clinging, to stop attaching. We are not, however, always seeing everything through *paññā* and this is why our defilements arise.

Part 2

The Four Noble Truths

"Samatha" (detail)
(oil on canvas [brown and gold], 80 cm x 106 cm.)
Tibor Novák (Hungary)

"Who here in this world is contented? Who has no agitations? What thinker knowing both sides, doesn't adhere in between? Whom do you call a great person? Who here has gone past the seamstress: craving?"

Venerable Tissa-Metteyya questions the Buddha[9]

5 Introduction

PEMASIRI THERA: There are four noble truths:

1. The truth of suffering, *dukkha-sacca*
2. The truth of the origin of suffering, *dukkha-samudaya-sacca*, which is craving, *taṇhā*
3. The truth of the extinction of suffering, *dukkha-nirodha-sacca*
4. The truth of the path leading to the extinction of suffering, *magga-sacca*, which is the eightfold path, *aṭṭhaṇgika-magga*

The four noble truths are a series of causes and effects. The second truth is the cause for the arising of the first: craving causes suffering. All our suffering arises out of craving for sensual pleasures, craving results from actions, and craving no result from actions. When there is no craving, there is no suffering. Similarly, the fourth truth is the cause for the arising of the third: the path ends suffering. This path is the eightfold path. When the eightfold path is followed, true knowledge arises, ignorance is destroyed, and suffering ends.

The four noble truths are truths, *saccāni*, because it is impossible to say suffering does not exist in the world, impossible to say craving does not cause suffering, impossible to say suffering cannot be extinguished, and impossible to say following the eightfold path will not end suffering. *Tatha*, *avitathāni*, *anaññathāni*. This Pali expression spoken by the Buddha means true, not untrue, and not otherwise—this is as it really is. The four noble truths are true, not untrue, and not otherwise. They are correct and accurate. Not one person in the world can successfully argue that these four statements are not facts. Not one person can change the truth of these four statements. The four noble truths are true.

The four noble truths are also noble, *ariya*. Noble is the way people who attain path and fruit see existence. They have a higher understanding of the nature of phenomena—see *anicca*, *dukkha*, and *anatta*—and have realised a stage of liberation from suffering. People are noble upon stream-entry. They cease to be worldly. All *arahats*, *pacceka-buddhas*, and *buddhas* are noble. *Arahats* follow the path laid out by the *buddhas* and realise the truths of existence. *Pacceka-buddhas* realise the truths by themselves, but cannot preach. *Pacceka-buddhas* are like mute people who see a dream: they cannot express their realisations. A *buddha* independently rediscovers and fully realises the truths of existence, and then proclaims these truths to the world.

Siddhārtha Gautama rediscovered and realised these truths of existence, attained complete liberation from suffering, and that is why he is a *buddha*. He attained enlightenment. He attained the highest possible position a human can attain. The four noble truths are noble because the Buddha, a fully enlightened and noble being, stated them.

The four noble truths are not conventional truths. Worldly men and women see the four noble truths from a worldly, mundane level; they see only four conventional truths of existence, *vohāra-sacca*. The truth of suffering, for example, is the first noble truth. Worldly people understand the first noble truth in terms that relate to their worldly experiences. They have not penetrated the true nature of suffering and therefore only understand the first truth as a conventional truth and not as a noble truth. Similarly, worldly people only understand the second, third, and fourth noble truths in worldly terms. They have not attained path and fruit, have not in fact penetrated these truths, and thus only understand them as conventional and not as noble truths. The four noble truths are hearsay for worldly people.

Noble people, on the other hand, do understand the four noble truths as noble truths. Because they have attained path and fruit, they see the four noble truths as ultimate truths, *paramattha-sacca*. A *sotāpanna*, for example, understands the truth of suffering as the noble truth of suffering because he or she has really penetrated the truth of suffering. He or she has gone beyond hearsay, beyond a conventional understanding of suffering, into an ultimate understanding. The *sotāpanna* understands the three other noble truths in the same way: he or she really penetrates the origin of suffering, the extinction of suffering, and the path leading to the extinction. Having attained realisation into the truth of the four noble truths, *sotāpanna*s and other noble people discuss the noble truths.

Children sometimes visit me. Wanting something to eat, they follow me to the kitchen, the pantry, and everywhere I go. I give them some chocolate and we talk about what is good and what is bad. I explain simple things to these children because that is all they understand. I do not try to explain the four noble truths to these children. No. These children do not understand this *dhamma*. The same for us. We only discuss the four truths, four conventional truths of existence, and we do not discuss the four noble truths. Instead, we discuss worldly suffering, worldly origins of suffering, worldly extinction of suffering, and worldly ways for the extinction of suffering. We talk about the four noble truths in an everyday way because we only see, at the beginning of our practice, four truths.

The Buddha taught both conventional and ultimate truths. He taught conventional truths to worldly people who wanted to reduce the suffering in their worldly lives and attain a fortunate birth in the human or in a heavenly world. Because these people had no interest in attaining *nibbāna*, he explained the nature of impermanence and only indirectly explained the nature of insubstantiality, of non-self. He explained to these people how they have to conduct themselves in this world to reduce their suffering in this world.

"Reduce your defilements," the Buddha told them. "Stop performing unwholesome actions, perform wholesome actions, and purify. This is what needs to be done." To worldly people, he did not teach the ultimate truth of the four noble truths. No.

Always seeing through the person, the Buddha taught according to the person's goals and abilities. He only taught ultimate truths to people who had the goal and ability to completely overcome all of their suffering, and attain *nibbāna*. What the Buddha taught depended upon the person whom he was teaching. Thus, he sometimes explained *dhamma* to attain a good birth, sometimes to attain *sotāpanna*, sometimes to attain *sakadāgāmī*, and sometimes to attain *arahatship*. We will know *dhamma*, know conventional and ultimate truths, and achieve our goals when our minds are pure. Meditative development is the way to *nibbāna*.

"Birth is suffering, ageing is suffering, sickness is suffering, death is suffering, sorrow and lamentation, pain, grief, and despair are suffering; association with the loathed is suffering, disassociation with the loved is suffering, not to get what one wants is suffering—in short, suffering is the five aggregates of clinging."

The Buddha—Dhammacakkappavattana Sutta[10]

6 Suffering

Pemasiri Thera: The first truth is suffering, *dukkha-sacca*. Suffering exists. No one can deny the existence of suffering. This statement is true, not untrue, and not otherwise. Even if I stand on my head, I cannot change the truth of this statement. Not one person can change the fact that suffering exists. This is solid, which is why the existence of suffering is called a truth. Suffering is the first truth.

It has four characteristics:

1. Oppression, *pīḷana*
2. Conditioned, *saṅkhata*
3. Heat and fire, *santāpa*
4. Change, *vipariṇāma*

Anything that has these four characteristics is called suffering.

When our minds are pure, the true nature of existence is clearly seen and we come to know our frustrations, pressures, and burdens. This is suffering's main characteristic: oppression. Arising out of causes, oppression is conditioned. Not just appearing out of nowhere, the suffering we experience arises because of a cause, and will not arise when there is no cause. There has to be a cause for suffering to arise. Suffering is the effect: we feel the oppression and the heat. Suffering burns. When we stand next to a fire, we feel heat. We can't say that we do not feel any heat when we stand near a fire. We definitely do feel heat near a fire. And finally, our suffering is at times extreme and at times fairly tolerable. It changes. All conditioned phenomena break up, which is suffering's characteristic of change. These four characteristics of suffering—oppression, conditioned, heat, and change—are true, not untrue, and not otherwise. *Tatha*, *avitathāni*, *anaññathāni*.

"And what, bhikkhus, is the noble truth of the origin of suffering? It is that craving which gives rise to birth, bound up with pleasure and passion, finding fresh delight now here, now there: that is to say craving for sensual pleasures, craving results from actions, and craving no results from actions. And where does this craving arise and establish itself? Wherever in the world there is anything agreeable and pleasurable, there craving arises and establishes itself."

The Buddha—Mahāsatipaṭṭhāna Sutta[11]

7 Origin of Suffering

PEMASIRI THERA: The second truth is the origin of suffering, *dukkha-samudaya-sacca*. Why do we suffer? Why is there unsatisfactoriness in our lives? What is the origin of our suffering?

The origin of suffering also has four characteristics:

1. Accumulates *kamma*, *āyūhana*
2. Creates the binding causal links of *saṃsāra*, *nidānȧ*
3. Bondage to suffering, *saṃyoga*
4. Obstacle to freedom from suffering, *palibodha*

Something with these four characteristics originates all kinds of suffering. As craving, *taṇhā*, has these four, it is the origin of suffering. Again, this statement is true, not untrue, and not otherwise.

Accumulates *kamma*, *āyūhana*, is the first characteristic of craving. The word accumulates is used in the sense of constructing and putting together. For example, by putting together bricks, concrete, rafters, and roof tiles in a specific manner, the workers here at our centre construct meditation huts. In the same way, by clinging, we construct our lives.

Saṃsāra is generally seen in terms of whole lives, going through one life after the other. Endlessly, the cycle of birth, aging and decay, death, and then again birth is repeated over and over again.

Though accepting the cycle of whole lives, wise people know life is a series of moments. When they perform an action in this moment, they know the good or bad result of their action is in the very next moment, while still in this life. Wise people know nothing from an action goes on to some indefinite future life. Each moment of their lives is a totally new and unique moment of mentality and materiality.

The composite nature of self, our minds and bodies, is summed up in the five aggregates of clinging, the *pañc'upādānakkhandha:* feelings, perceptions, volitional formations, consciousness, and materiality.

By putting together the causes for the arising of the five aggregates of clinging in one moment, the five aggregates are experienced as a self in the next moment. We are continually putting together the causes for the arising of the five aggregates. From the time we get up in the morning until the time we go to bed at night, we crave pleasant sights, sounds, smells, tastes, physical contacts, and thoughts. We rarely restrain ourselves from pleasant contact with sense objects. Quite the opposite. We try to find new delight in them.

Because an *arahat* stops putting together the causes for the arising of the five aggregates of clinging, he or she never takes birth again.

David: If an *arahat* stops putting together the causes for the arising of the five aggregates, why do the five aggregates continue to arise? Why doesn't an *arahat* vanish?

Reproductive *kamma*, *janaka-kamma*, is strong and it continues to produce the five aggregates for the duration of an *arahat*'s life span. Only clinging to the five aggregates has stopped. No more clinging for an *arahat*. That's all. Without clinging, an *arahat* has no sense of self—just bides his or her time, fully mindful, craving neither life nor death.

Because *anāgāmis* stop putting together the causes for the arising of the aggregates of the sense-sphere realm, they never again take birth in the sense-sphere realm, the *kāma-loka*. *Sotāpanna*s stop putting together the causes for the arising of the aggregates of the lower planes of existence, the *apāyas*, which means they never take birth in the *apāyas*. They only take birth in the higher planes of existence.

The next characteristic of the origin of suffering, of craving, is its creating the binding causal links, the *nidāna*, of *saṃsāra*. There are twelve chief causes and effects that perpetuate our existence in *saṃsāra*: (1) ignorance, (2) volitional formations, (3) consciousness, (4) mentality-materiality, (5) six sense-bases, (6) contact, (7) feelings, (8) craving, (9) clinging, (10) renewed existence, (11) birth, and (12) decay and death.

With craving being the link between these mental and material causes and effects, it is craving that is constantly supplying the source for our suffering. When we crave pleasant contact with objects, we also create the link to suffering. We are inclined to crave the pleasant. By constantly following our inclinations and expanding our craving, we are also constantly creating the very strong causal links that bind us in *saṃsāra*. Our craving feeds our suffering. We supply the source for our own suffering.

The third characteristic of craving is its association with suffering. Craving is our bondage, *saṃyoga*, to suffering. During our lifetimes, we have all performed many wholesome and also many unwholesome actions. Many of our actions perpetuated our suffering and hindered our progress towards the attainment of *nibbāna*.

Do wholesome actions hinder my progress?

When you are attached to the performance of wholesome actions, you prevent the complete extinction of suffering and the attainment of *nibbāna*. Attachment obstructs your liberation. If you perform many wholesome actions, you can be born as a *deva*, a *brahma*, or again as a human being. If you perform many weak and unwholesome actions, you might be born as a snake or some other form of animal.

*Sotāpanna*s have a different quality of bondage from worldly people: they have reduced their bondage and eliminated the possibility of taking birth in a lower realm. When *sotāpanna*s attain to the *sakadāgāmī* stage, their bondage is further changed and reduced. There are even more changes and reductions for *anāgāmi*s. *Arahats* have extinguished all bondage. Because we are craving contact with pleasant objects and are attached to the performance of wholesome actions, we are still in bondage. Misunderstanding wholesome and unwholesome actions, we associate with suffering and fail to attain *nibbāna*.

The fourth characteristic of craving is its obstruction to freedom from suffering, *palibodha*. Craving is an obstacle to *nibbāna*. Throughout our lives, we crave the five aggregates. We cling to them. This hoarding of mentality and materiality results in our deaths. Because these aggregates belong to us, we have to die and then be born again. We are working for our deaths.

Working for our deaths sounds odd.

The Buddha saw the world completely opposite to the way we normally see the world. He worked for the deathless. The Buddha did not work for death. It is not a problem of living; it is a problem of dying. That is the problem. When nothing remains in our stores, there is no need for us to die and take birth. The Buddha gained freedom from birth precisely because nothing remained in his stores. By completely extinguishing his craving, he escaped dying. When there is no craving, there is no dying. We are always working for our deaths and fail to, as the Buddha did, work for the deathless. We dislike working for the deathless because that is the path of purification—meditative development. But by meditating properly, we gain freedom from death.

When we look at the space directly in front of where we are sitting, we cannot see anything. But because we know air is materially present in that space, we do not say the space is empty. Similarly, we do not see the craving in our minds. It is only when we contact a particularly pleasant or unpleasant object with our senses that we become aware of our habitual, though latent, craving for that pleasant or unpleasant object. Only when the object actually enters our minds do we become aware of how craving is continually born. Ignorance of our craving and its consequences is a huge obstacle.

To overcome this obstacle, meditators investigate the nature and drawbacks of craving. Upon investigation, they find that craving is the origin of suffering. Craving causes suffering. Wanting to end suffering, wanting to attain *nibbāna*, meditators are mindful of craving. They break their attachment to the process.

"The wise ones, ever meditative and steadfastly persevering, alone experience nibbāna—the incomparable freedom from bondage."

The Buddha—Dhammapada[12]

8 Extinction of Suffering

Pemasiri Thera: The third truth is extinction of suffering, *dukkha-nirodha-sacca. Nirodha* means extinction. It is the opposite of origination, *samudaya.* Extinction is the end. It is the complete destruction of causes. No results or effects originate from extinction. Anything that becomes extinct is completely destroyed, never to arise or exist again. It is not extinction when you lose something because you can find what you lost.

Loss and complete destruction are two different events. If we die, we will be born again. If we do not die, attain extinction of suffering, there is nothing to be born again. Some people believe in a soul that lives on after the physical death of the body. They believe extinction of suffering must be heaven where the soul lives in peace for all eternity. This is not what is meant by extinction of suffering. All forms of conditioned phenomena are subject to decay and death, and thus they originate suffering. A soul living in a peaceful heaven, even as some type of invisible entity, is still a form of conditioned phenomenon. Hence, life in a heaven must still originate suffering. *Nirodha* means the complete extinction of suffering. *Nirodha* means decay, death, and birth will never come again. *Tatha, avitathāni, anaññathāni.*

The extinction of suffering has four characteristics, being:

1. An escape from suffering, *nissaraṇa*
2. Free from disturbance, *viveka*
3. Unconditioned, *asaṅkhata*
4. Deathlessness, *amata*

Only *nibbāna* has all four of these characteristics.

The first characteristic of extinction is its being an escape from suffering, *nissaraṇa.* Escape means our minds are pure, free of defilements. What are defilements?

David: You once said defilements are our mental garbage.

Defilements, *kilesa*, are unwholesome qualities that soil our minds. Defiling a mind requires the existence of a being, a *satta*. A being exists because of attachment and ceases to exist if there is no attachment. Thus, when there is no being, there are no defilements. The mind is pure when there is no being.

You see my teacup. Who craves it? Who is attached to it? Is the person who owns the teacup attached to the teacup or is someone else attached to it?

The person who owns it.

The process that leads to the defilements arising begins as soon as the teacup enters the picture. Once the teacup is offered to me, I can crave and be attached to it. All of us can become attached to things when we know they belong to us, and then they can make us unhappy. Picture the time when this teacup did not exist. The teacup has yet to be made and no one has given it to me. What is in my mind at that time? If I have not been offered the teacup, would I be craving for it? Would I be attached to it?

No.

Before the teacup exists, there is no attachment to it. I neither crave the teacup nor am I attached to it before the idea of the teacup enters my mind. There is no craving and no clinging whatsoever. With regard to this particular teacup, nothing arises in my mind. This is what the characteristic of the escape from suffering, *nissaraṇa*, and the characteristic of the extinction state of mind, *nirodha*, are like. What will you tell someone who asks you to explain escaping from suffering and *nirodha*?

I will tell them about their car. I'd ask if they remember the time when they were children and didn't have a car. At that time, they weren't attached to it and didn't have any car problems.

If no one ever makes a car, where is the craving? Where is the attachment?

It isn't there.

If anything exists, there is suffering. If nothing exists, then extinction. No suffering. If the five aggregates exist, there is attachment to the five aggregates and thus there is suffering. If nothing exists, there is no suffering. There is only the extinction, *nirodha*.

The second characteristic of extinction is its being free from disturbance, *viveka*. Generally, when people in Sri Lanka refer to *viveka*, being free from disturbance, they mean rest, taking a break from work and doing very little.

Children, for example, say their father is in *viveka* when he is on holiday. The father relaxes, reads a newspaper, smokes a cigarette, and thinks about this and that. Taking a holiday from work is what we generally refer to as *viveka*. But when Buddha referred to *viveka*, he meant something else.

"*Viveka*," said the Buddha, "is an emptiness of defilements."

Actually, the father is not particularly free from disturbance while on holiday because he continues to disturb his mind: he generates defilements and carries a load. Being free from disturbance isn't even found in *jhāna* because there is still some weight, some disturbance, in the *jhāna* state. In the sense-sphere realm, *kāma-loka*, the average person weighs their mind down with thoughts of sensual pleasures: food, a car, house, child, husband or wife, or some form of property. But the *jhāna*, the mental absorption, also has its form of weight. The person who attains to the first *jhāna*, for example, may try to possess the *jhāna* factors of applied and sustained thought, rapture, happiness, and one-pointedness. He or she may crave and be attached to these mental factors. They are different disturbances and loads from those found in the sense-sphere realm, but they are still disturbances and loads. The person who attains *jhāna* can take birth in the immaterial realm or even become a *mahā-brahmā*, but there is still some disturbance and load.

Siddhārtha strove to gain complete freedom from all disturbances and loads.

Little by little, we also try to unload the defilements that disturb and burden our minds. Slowly, we gain more freedom from disturbance, more *viveka*. Little by little, we gain more freedom, more detachment, more unloading, more freedom from disturbance, and so on and so forth. The *sotāpanna* unloads many of his or her burdens. If we become *arahats*, we unload all of our burdens. We gain freedom from disturbance, are really in *viveka*, when we completely unload all of our defilements. We then say we are resting. That is real relaxation. Anyone who lives without defilements is resting and is free from disturbance. This is true, not untrue, and not otherwise. Nobody can change it. This is the truth.

The next characteristic of extinction, *dukkha-nirodha*, is the unconditioned, *asaṅkhata*. *Dukkha* has the characteristic of being conditioned, *saṅkhata*, whereas extinction has the characteristic of being unconditioned, *asaṅkhata*. In the conditioned, there are causes and effects, *hetu-phala*. In the unconditioned, there is no cause and thus no effect. In this world, we can find only two things that are unconditioned: space and *nibbāna*.

We generally refer to the gap between two objects as space. But the gap between two objects is not the space I am now referring to. The space I am referring to is called *ākāsa* in Pali. *Ākāsa* is different because, unlike the air type of space between our thumbs and forefingers, *ākāsa* never changes, decays, or dies. *Ākāsa* never arises and no one can ever steal it though we cannot say it is empty. These are also the qualities we can find in *nibbāna*.

There are no obstructions in space. In the space of the sky, we see how the birds are flying. In the space of the unconditioned, in *nibbāna*, the *arahats* are flying and not the birds. That's the only change we have to make. So it is with *asaṅkhata*.

Tell me, why do we call this world beautiful?

DAVID: The world arouses pleasant feelings. I like it.

STUDENT #2: Because we are deluded, we see sensual pleasures as beautiful.

I think space is what makes the world beautiful. When there is enough space, a dancer performs beautifully. And when there is enough space, we build a new home. It is not the home that is beautiful. No. Space is what enables the home to be beautiful. In the space of the unconditioned, there are no causes and no effects—no *hetu-phala*—and therefore no trouble or suffering. We only find trouble where we find causes and effects, in the conditioned.

Before the time of the Buddha, many teachers of meditation worked to discover a level of consciousness that was beyond causes and effects, and therefore beyond suffering. Instead, they found levels of consciousness with causes and effects, and thus with suffering. The Buddha discovered *nirodha*. Beyond all causes and effects, *nirodha* is beyond suffering. *Nirodha* is the unconditioned, *nibbāna*.

The fourth characteristic of the extinction of suffering is deathlessness, *amata*. *Mata* means death. All conditioned things eventually break up and disappear. If there is a cause and an effect, there must be death. *Amata* means no death, the deathless. In extinction, there is no cause and no effect, which means there is nothing to die. As before, this is true, not untrue, and not otherwise. This is unalterable, as it really is.

"In the first watch of the night, ignorance was banished and true knowledge arose, darkness was banished and light arose, as happens in one who abides diligent, ardent, and resolute."

The Buddha—Bhayabherava Sutta[13]

9 Path Leading to the Extinction of Suffering

Pemasiri Thera: The fourth truth is the path that leads to the extinction of suffering, *magga-sacca*. This path is the eightfold path, *aṭṭhaṅgika-magga*: right understanding, right thought, right speech, right action, right livelihood, right effort, right mindfulness, and right concentration. This is the path of meditative development. It leads to *nibbāna*. *Tatha*, *avitathāni*, *anaññathāni*.

The eightfold path has four characteristics:

1. Leads to release and deliverance, *niyyāna*
2. Is a cause for the attainment of *arahatship*, *hetu*
3. Seeing the four noble truths, *dassana*
4. Overcomes craving and attains mastery over oneself, *adhipati*

Release

The first characteristic of the eightfold path is its assistance in delivering us from suffering. Leading to our release, *niyyāna*, the eightfold path is a raft we use to cross the river of *saṃsāra*. If we attain to *sotāpanna*, we are free from wrong understanding, no longer cling to rituals, and have no doubt about the spiritual practice.

Some people are confused about the practice. They know *sīla* is important. They know their mental development requires abstinence, *virati*, from inappropriate conduct, and they also know that sometimes they must make great effort to abstain from inappropriate conduct. *Āyati saṃvara sīla* helps people train in appropriate conduct and helps them refrain from indulging in inappropriate conduct. *Sīla* is the foundation for meditative development, but sometimes people take it to the extreme.

I know a *bhikkhu* who ignored a large sore on his shoulder. Instead of attending to it, he let it fester, bore the pain, and hurt his body because he felt he should punish his body. His behaviour did not in any way help him to progress. This is not *sīla*. He is holding onto wrong views and indulging in some form of self-mortification. He is simply practising the eightfold path improperly. Appropriate conduct, *sīla*, is the middle way. It has no connection with self-mortification. *Sīla* means we restrain our words and actions.

Because of previous unwholesome actions, we do sometimes experience unwholesome results, *vipāka*; we can even take birth in a hell, an animal realm, or a *peta-loka*. But if we enter the stream, all of our unwholesome *kamma* that is destined to take effect in future births becomes ineffective, has no opportunity to yield results. When we attain to *sotāpanna*, the first stage of liberation, we cross halfway to the other shore. We will never be born again in a lower world and the number of future births is already limited. And the *sotāpanna* only takes birth in happy courses of existence, such as the human or heavenly worlds. He or she is no longer aimlessly drifting in *saṃsāra*. Attaining to *sotāpanna* leads to release, *niyyāna*.

DAVID: Is the number of future births limited to seven?

There are suttas stating that *sotāpanna*s are limited to seven future births. The number of births, however, is unlimited for the average worldly person. We cannot say there are just a few more births, as there is no limit to this process. We know not where these births originated and know not where they are going to end. *Saṃsāra* is endless suffering.

One of the characteristics of the origin of suffering, of craving, is its obstruction to freedom. Craving is an obstacle, a *palibodha*, to attaining extinction from suffering. Due to craving, we defile our minds with greed, aversion, and delusion. These three unwholesome roots—greed, aversion, and delusion—include everything that obstructs our freedom. Compare the rich man to the poor beggar:

"I," the rich man says, "have many problems in my life, but a beggar's life is free. He has no problems. He only has to beg whenever he is hungry, only needs a tree to sleep under, and sleeps whenever he likes. I cannot live in that way. I have to work very hard. The beggar definitely has far fewer problems than I do."

The beggar says exactly the same thing.

"I have many problems in my life, but a rich man has no problems in his. The rich man does not have to beg because he has enough money to buy food and he does not have to sleep under a tree because he has a comfortable bed in his luxurious home. The rich man has no problems whatsoever."

Both the rich man and the beggar say exactly the same thing. They both say they have many problems, but the other man has no problems. The truth is both the rich man and the beggar have problems, as everyone in the world has problems. To solve their problems, many people come to see us *bhikkhus*. Some have minor problems at work, some have problems at home, and some are ill and dying. People come to see us because they think we can help them. Many ask us to tie a string around their wrists, perform a *pūjā*, bless some oil, or make an offering to the Bodhi Tree. They believe rituals will help ease their suffering, but most often rituals fail to do so. And when rituals fail, they pass judgement on the Buddha's teachings: "Buddhism is useless. We get nothing from it."

There are many misconceptions of the four noble truths and *dhamma*. Wealth, for example, does not guarantee happiness nor does poverty guarantee misery. Even a poor beggar can attain extinction. And secondly, people will fail to escape suffering by just having a string tied around their wrists or by having someone bless some oil. These are low-level aspects of Buddhism and have little to do with what the Buddha taught. The Buddha explained the nature of reality.

"To ease your suffering," said the Buddha, "you must understand the nature of your problems, the nature of your suffering, and the nature of your mind."

Anyone who fully understands, through personal experience, their obstacles to gaining freedom from suffering can destroy their obstacles and gain freedom. People who never try to understand their own minds will never have any success in destroying obstacles or in escaping suffering.

Cause

The second characteristic of the eightfold path is its being a cause, a *hetu*, for the extinction of suffering. Initially, we all have many obstacles, *palibodha*, to properly practising the eightfold path. When we begin the practice, it is difficult to maintain proper *sīla* because we have many obstacles in our daily lives to maintaining *sīla*. At the beginning, we also have many obstacles to attaining proper *samādhi* and many obstacles to developing *paññā*. Initially, there are always many, many obstacles to properly practising the eightfold path. But by gradually reducing these obstacles, we also gradually develop our ability to properly practise the eightfold path. This is an ongoing process and it takes some effort.

Many people, however, are reluctant to make anything more than a modest effort in practising *dhamma* because they feel any greater effort will disrupt their family life. They are mistaken. Visākhā was a woman who lived at the time of the Buddha. She made the effort to practise the *dhamma* properly, destroyed her obstacles to freedom, and attained stream-entry position when she was just seven years old. She married at sixteen and subsequently gave birth to twenty children. She was also very wealthy. Her wedding dress alone cost a small fortune. How can people say that practising the *dhamma* disrupts family life if someone like Visākhā was able to raise twenty children—ten boys and ten girls—while she practised the *dhamma*?

The person who makes the right effort destroys many obstacles and attains to *sotāpanna*. In subsequent happy courses of existence, the *sotāpanna* becomes stronger and stronger. He or she gradually increases the quality of their *sīla* as well as gradually increasing their powers of *samādhi* and *paññā*. The *sotāpanna* steadily increases the power of the eightfold path and the power of the four foundations of mindfulness. *Sotāpanna*s increase their striving effort, roads-to-power, spiritual faculties, and the seven factors of enlightenment. *Sotāpanna*s gradually develop and increase all of these powers. The development of these powers is the root cause, the *hetu*, for attaining *arahatship*. This is what we have to develop.

Seeing

The next characteristic of the eightfold path is seeing the four noble truths, *dassana*. We clearly see our defilements. There is nothing else to clearly see, but our defilements. If defilements are clearly seen, we will gain freedom from them. When we gain insight into the true nature of defilements, we eradicate them. We destroy our defilements through seeing, through *dassana*.

Because we turned the lights on, the room we are in is quite bright. How long did it take for the light to overcome the darkness?

Almost no time at all. It's instantaneous.

Where did the darkness go?

I don't know.

It is difficult to know where darkness goes. Imagine yourself in a dense jungle. It is raining heavily, it is midnight, and it is a new moon day, which means no light shines from the moon. You are in the depths of this pitch-black darkness when suddenly—a flash of lightening! The bright flash immediately allows you to see something. You see snakes, elephants, and many other wild animals, and it is clear the jungle is dangerous and is no place to live. Wanting to escape, you immediately take a step forward. Taking that one step forward means you are halfway out of the dark and dangerous jungle. You are halfway to eradicating your defilements: you have become a *sotāpanna*.

Because the defilements that arose in our past are dead, we cannot do anything about them. We also cannot do anything about defilements that will arise in our future because they do not as yet exist. We can only do something about defilements that are arising here and now. The practice of *vipassanā* means being in the present. *Vipassanā* means we do not think nor worry about what has happened in the past, it means we do not think nor worry about the future, and it also means we do not cling in this very moment to anything at all. This was the advice the Buddha gave to Commander Santati. Do you know the story?

No.

Commander Santati won a battle for King Kosala. To honour Santati, the King gave a celebration with many dancers, music, food, and drink. Santati greatly enjoyed himself at this celebration and was particularly fond of one dancer. He really enjoyed her. The dancer, however, collapsed from exhaustion during one of her performances and died right in front of Santati. Her death came without warning and was a great shock for Santati. He immediately left the celebration and went to the Buddha for guidance.

"Drop the present," the Buddha told Santati. "Drop thinking about the past, drop thinking about the future, and do not cling to anything in this very moment."

Santati was a wise person. He immediately understood the Buddha's teaching, gained insight—*dassana*—and attained enlightenment. He needed only a few words from the Buddha to see the true nature of his condition. "Commander Santati," said the Buddha that very morning, "is a wise person. He will be an *arahat* by this evening."

From the time of the Buddha, there are many similar stories. One day, the Buddha visited a skilled acrobat named Uggasena who was performing feats on top of a bamboo pole. When the Buddha had Uggasena's attention, he told him the same thing he had told Santati: "Drop the present. Drop thinking about the past, drop thinking about the future, and do not cling to anything in this very moment." While still on the pole, Uggasena immediately gained insight and attained enlightenment. Uggasena was another wise person who lived at the time of the Buddha.

There are wise people in our society.

You are correct. There are wise people in today's society, but the Buddha's message is not getting through to them. Thus, many people practise sitting and walking meditation for years, for decades, and for whole lifetimes without making any real gains. But Santati and Uggasena got the message. They listened carefully to the Buddha's advice and as a result gained *dassana*, attained enlightenment in just a few seconds. Teachers direct us. They let us know that if we look into the night sky in this and that direction, we will see stars and planets. When we look in the direction the teacher suggests, we do see stars and planets. If we have the wisdom to look in the right direction, we clearly see with our own eyes and gain liberation. A *sotāpanna* looked in the right direction. He or she penetrated the nature of reality, destroyed their doubt, and attained realisation into the truth of the four noble truths. *Sotāpanna*s experience *dassana*.

Mastery

The fourth characteristic of the eightfold path is the overcoming of craving and the attaining of mastery over oneself, *adhipati*. *Adhipati* translates as dominance and predominance. It is master.

There are many types of masters. There are masters in workplaces, nature, and on the path leading to the extinction of suffering. Strong administrators are masters of their employees. Even though some employees have their own opinions on how a job should be performed, they comply with the strong administrator's way. The sea is a master in nature. Streams and rivers begin in various countries and flow in many directions, but eventually they all flow to the sea. And despite such a large volume of fresh water flowing from the rivers into the sea, the saltiness of the sea is never altered. An enormous body of salty water, the sea remains very salty, forever. The sea is master of streams and rivers. All streams and rivers flow to the sea. Path knowledge, *magga-ñāṇa*, is master in our lives. On the path leading to the extinction of suffering, it is master.

There can be only one master; only one person can be master of one workplace at any one time. If two people both think they are master of the same workplace, conflicts and problems arise. A workplace only runs peacefully when one administrator, one master, is completely in charge. When employees follow their administrator's way and let go of their own way, everything flows smoothly. Still, some human masters definitely do cause problems for people and society.

But there are masters that never cause any problems for anything or anyone. The sea is one of these masters. All the streams and rivers in the world flow smoothly towards it. The sea is their master, entirely. The master we work for is path knowledge. Making the eightfold path predominant in our lives, path knowledge never causes us any problems either. Restraining our sense doors, practising *sīla*, practising generosity, living in the present moment, practising *vipassanā*—everything we do is done to attain mastery over ourselves and attain path knowledge. Just like streams that flow to the sea without problem, the eightfold path is the stream we follow to reduce our problems, live peacefully, and reach the sea of path knowledge.

The next time you go down to the sea take a few moments to reflect on its nature. The sea only gradually gets deeper and deeper: quite shallow near the shoreline, small birds walk; a little farther out to sea, children wade up to their waists; and way out to sea, the sharks and whales are swimming and playing. Sharks and whales are found way out to sea because, in the watery depths where the sea extends far below the surface, they have enough room to perform any activity. The sea starts shallow, but it gets deeper and deeper. The sea is deep.

To end our suffering, we need to answer four questions:

1. What is suffering?
2. What is the origin of suffering?
3. What is the extinction of suffering?
4. What is the path leading to the extinction of suffering?

When through our own experience we answer these four questions satisfactorily, we reduce our obstacles to freedom, reduce our troubles, and reduce our suffering.

2,500 years ago Siddhārtha set out to answer these questions. He set out to discover what is wholesome and what is truth. He finally rediscovered these four truths of existence, fully realised these truths, and then, as the Buddha, proclaimed these truths to the world. This is very important. People who have the correct understanding, *sammā-diṭṭhi*, of the Buddha's teachings will always have fewer problems and less suffering than those who don't. We can only just begin to appreciate the Buddha. He was a person who applied himself, made these discoveries independently, and attained complete liberation from suffering.

Part 3

The Noble Eightfold Path

Untitled
(Paper and ink, 11cm. by 8cm.)
Tamara Jayasuriya (Sri Lanka)

"The sage who makes an effort in truth doesn't fall back."

The Buddha—Ādhipateyya Sutta[14]

10 Introduction

Pemasiri Thera: *Ariya-aṭṭhaṇgika magga*: *ariya* means noble; *aṭṭha*, eight; *angika*, group or fold; *magga*, path. *Ariya-aṭṭhangika-magga*: the noble eightfold path. It has eight factors:

1. Right Understanding, *sammā-diṭṭhi*
2. Right Thought, *sammā-saṅkappa*
3. Right Speech, *sammā-vācā*
4. Right Action, *sammā-kammanta*
5. Right Livelihood, *sammā-ājīva*
6. Right Effort, *sammā-vāyāma*
7. Right Mindfulness, *sammā-sati*
8. Right Concentration, *sammā-samādhi*

People who really walk the noble eightfold path have no faults and see cause and effect in all of their actions.

Sometimes, we develop only one or two factors of the eightfold path. We may, for example, have a well-developed understanding of the teachings, but our concentration is poor. Or our effort and self-discipline may be high, such as when we are offering alms, but our other factors may be low. I am not saying offering alms is wrong; that is the normal practice. I am saying it is important to work at balancing all eight factors when engaged in any activity. We may not even balance all eight while living in a meditation centre. To balance all eight factors and progress, we have to meditate.

"When a noble disciple understands the unwholesome and the root of the unwholesome, the wholesome and the root of the wholesome, he or she is of right understanding."

Venerable Sāriputta—Sammādiṭṭhi Sutta[15]

11 Right Understanding

PEMASIRI THERA: The first factor of the noble eightfold path is right understanding, *sammā-diṭṭhi*. The word *sammā* is important. Meaning noble and only applying to a Buddha, *sammā* is the highest possible position a human can attain. Noble ones understand the way, clearly see the path, and destroy all defilements. They understand the *ariyan* truths. They live peaceful and harmonious lives, never intend to harm, never find any joy in harming.

Right understanding is understanding the four noble truths:

1. Understanding suffering, *dukkha-ñāṇa*
2. Understanding the origin of suffering, *dukkha-samudaya-ñāṇa*, which means understanding craving, *taṇhā*
3. Understanding the extinction of suffering, *dukkha-nirodha-ñāṇa*
4. Understanding the path leading to the extinction of suffering, *magga-ñāṇa*, which means understanding the eightfold path, *aṭṭhangika-magga*

Be aware that right understanding and the four noble truths share the same four factors: suffering, origin, extinction, and path. When examining right understanding, we have to remember what we learned about the four noble truths. We have to remember the fourth truth of the four noble truths is the eightfold path, and we have to remember the first factor of the eightfold path is an understanding of the four noble truths. The eightfold path and the four noble truths are interconnected. When right understanding arises, there is no room in the heart for craving.

"An instructed disciple of the noble ones reflects in this way: I am now being chewed up by feeling. But in the past I was also chewed up by feeling in the same way I am now being chewed up by present feeling. And if I delight in future feeling, then in the future I will be chewed up by feeling in the same way I am now being chewed up by present feeling."

The Buddha—Khajjaniya Sutta[16]

12 Right Thought

PEMASIRI THERA: The second factor of the eightfold path is right thought, *sammā-saṅkappa*. *Saṅkappa* is also translated as intention. There are three kinds of right thoughts:

1. Thoughts of renunciation and generosity, *nekkhamma-saṅkappa*
2. Thoughts of good will and loving-kindness, *avyāpāda-saṅkappa*
3. Thoughts of harmlessness and compassion, *avihiṃsā-saṅkappa*

Thoughts of renunciation are free from greed and craving for sensual pleasures; thoughts of good will and loving-kindness are for the welfare of all beings; thoughts of harmlessness and compassion are for the non-injury of all beings.

Kindness, compassion, generosity, wisdom—these factors are the basis for proper renunciation. We sometimes practise renunciation when we are angry. We dislike something, even hate it, and want to escape. This is not proper renunciation. No. Proper renunciation only ever arises out of wisdom. When we have wisdom, we also have kindness and compassion. As a result, we turn away from craving for sensual pleasures and turn towards renunciation. Thinking it was unreasonable for Prince Siddhārtha to leave his wife and new-born son, many people criticise Siddhārtha's renunciation of the worldly life at Kapilavatthu. But his renunciation of the worldly life was based on wisdom. It was a kind and compassionate action.

DAVID: I agree with being kind and compassionate. But why would I want to renounce family and friends, like Siddhārtha did?

The practice is not about renouncing people. If you read the Bodhi Jātakas, you find descriptions of Prince Siddhārtha's life with Princess Yasodhara. Siddhārtha and Yasodhara lived together as husband and wife for thirteen years at Kapilavatthu. "As a couple," said the Buddha, "we exchanged ideas and knew each other's minds."

Yasodhara knew that her husband was a very unusual man, knew what he had seen for his life, and was prepared for his renunciation. She helped him with his renunciation. The *bodhisatta* Siddhārtha did not simply reject his family and run off. No. His renunciation of the worldly life was a decision made in consultation with Yasodhara; it was a joint decision made over their years together as a couple. There are accounts in the Jātakas of how she gave him the fullest support. She was a devoted and faithful wife. You must have read the story of the Buddha returning to Kapilavatthu for the first time after his enlightenment. Yasodhara spots the Buddha walking along a road with thousands of *bhikkhus*. "Look," said Yasodhara to their seven-year-old son Rāhula, "here comes your father. He is a handsome and great man. He is a lion among men."

Yasodhara's comments reveal her affection for her former husband; there is no trace of anger towards the Buddha. If Prince Siddhārtha had simply rejected her and run off, those feelings of affection towards the Buddha would not have been displayed. She respected and understood Siddhārtha's decision to renounce the worldly life. It was a decision based on wisdom.

I am holding a teacup. You know what this teacup looks like because you are looking at it with your own eyes. You can clearly see this teacup. In the same way, we come to understand the four noble truths when we look at the four noble truths. We start by looking to see if the existence of suffering is a truth in our own experience. When we manage to look clearly, we do see that we are suffering; thus, the wise course of action is to do what we can to ease our suffering. It is only after we gain some understanding of the reality of suffering that we in fact begin to develop any real intention to gain freedom from suffering. Clearly seeing the four noble truths, right thoughts and intentions arise. This is wisdom. If we are to gain liberation, wisdom is essential.

Right thoughts are of renunciation, kindness, and compassion. We must first have some kindness and compassion for ourselves before we can spread kindness and compassion to others. If we cannot be kind to ourselves, how can we possibly be kind to others? If we cannot even ease our own suffering, how can we ease the suffering of others? Kindness and compassion for others are only possible when we genuinely feel kindness and compassion for ourselves. Our intention to find happiness and gain freedom from suffering—for ourselves—is of primary importance. We must first cross over the river before we can help others to cross over.

Mahouts keep their elephants captive with iron chains. To gain freedom, strong elephants break their chains with their trunks and then return to the jungle. We are held captive in suffering by wrong thoughts, which arise out of our greed, aversion, and delusion. To gain freedom from our suffering, we use right thoughts to replace wrong thoughts. Right thoughts are those that arise out of loving-kindness, compassion, and renunciation. Thoughts of kindness and compassion replace thoughts of cruelty and coldness, hatred and harm; thoughts of renunciation and generosity replace thoughts of greed and craving for sensual pleasures; and thoughts to perform wholesome actions replace thoughts to perform unwholesome actions. When we are free from unwholesome thoughts, we gain freedom from suffering, from *saṃsāra*.

You frequently help a meditator at this centre who injured her arm in a motorcycle accident. Observers think you have a lot of kindness and compassion for this meditator and are simply helping her. You too even think you are just trying to free this person from her suffering. This is delusion. Helping this woman is a good action that arises out of kindness and compassion; therefore, it is an action performed with right thought. But your kindness and compassion are actually directed towards yourself and not towards this injured woman. When you see this woman suffering, you are also suffering.

Yes. I get sharp pains in my belly.

You can clearly see those pains. They are internal phenomena, not something external. When she feels pressure, you feel pressure; when she suffers, you suffer. By trying to ease her feelings of pain, you are trying to ease your pain. You are trying to escape your own suffering by helping her. That is what you are doing.

Generally, people won't grasp or even want to accept this idea—some outright reject it. Many state that it is improper to relate to people in this way and only accept relationships with other people on a fifty-fifty basis. Fifty-fifty is good enough for most people. If you exceed the fifty-fifty ratio, go beyond an equal give and take relationship, they say you are on the wrong path.

Money, praise, fame, pleasure—something is normally expected from the performance of an action. If people do not expect to make some money or elevate their status, some other form of benefit is expected. When, however, an action is performed completely out of generosity, kindness, and compassion, there is no expectation for any form of benefit, none whatsoever. Performing actions without expectations is true renunciation.

How can our society function without expectations? Don't criminals have to be punished for their crimes?

The human world is sometimes very bad and sometimes very good. Some people are like devils while others are kind and compassionate. Good and bad forms of behaviour exist. Compassionate teachers explain to us that it is better to do this and better to not do that. The teacher clearly explains the nature of the world. But even when compassionate teachers speak, only a few people listen and actually follow their teachings. Most do not. This is the nature of the world. Teachers can only explain things. They cannot force people to behave in a certain way.

Not even the Buddha could control the actions of his own *saṅgha*, let alone the whole world. At one time in his *saṅgha*, there was a major disagreement over which rules of discipline must be compulsory. *Bhikkhus* argued over the proposed changes and split into two divisions. The Buddha returned to the forest. Some people fight. Some people choose to live in harmony.

The beautiful *bhikkhuni* Uppalavaṇṇā, a contemporary of the Buddha, lived on her own in the forest. Infatuated by the *bhikkhuni's* beauty, a young shepherd of the area sneaked into her *kuṭi* while she was on alms round. When Uppalavaṇṇā returned, he attacked and raped her. She screamed, protested, and begged him to stop. She did everything she could to get him to stop his attack, but he continued. Even in the face of such cruelty, Uppalavaṇṇā maintained her compassion for the shepherd. Understanding the nature of cause and effect, she was wise. But the shepherd was foolish. As a result of his cruel actions, he was dragged into a hell.

Right thought is an important topic that needs a great deal of discussion. By clearly seeing the four noble truths, we clearly see right thought.

"That being so, Ānanda, remember this too as a wonderful and marvellous quality of the Tathāgatha: here, Ānanda, for the Tathāgatha feelings are known as they arise, as they are present, as they disappear; perceptions are known as they arise, as they are present, as they disappear; thoughts are known as they arise, as they are present, as they disappear. Remember this too, Ānanda, as a wonderful and marvellous quality of the Tathāgatha."

The Buddha—Acchariya-abbhuta Sutta[17]

13 Right Speech

PEMASIRI THERA: The third factor of the eightfold path is right speech, *sammā-vācā*. With a degree of wisdom, which means first establishing right understanding and right thought, we use our power of speech, our voices, wholesomely and appropriately. In terms of cause and effect, dependent upon the right understanding of the four truths as the cause, right thought arises. And then dependent upon right thought, our kindness and compassion, right speech arises. If we are to speak appropriately, wisdom is crucial. We need to use words that always bring people together. We speak:

- The truth
- Words of friendship and harmony
- Words of kindness, sympathy, and comfort
- Words of encouragement
- Words that benefit

And we must abstain from using words in ways that disturb the freedom of people. We abstain from:

- False speech, *musā-vāda*
- Slanderous speech, *pisuṇā-vācā*
- Harsh and abusive speech, *pharusā-vācā*
- Gossip and idle chatter, *samphappalāpa*

All are forms of inappropriate speech.

False speech is to speak untruths that deceive other people. You find this form of speech in politics, in theatre, and also sometimes in preaching. Fortunetellers, who earn their living forecasting the future, use magical and surprising words that deceive people. These fortunetellers know nothing about their customers' lives, but they slyly obtain that information saying that this and that will happen. It is false speech.

Slanderous speech means pointing out another person's faults with the intention of alienating that person from another person. It is malicious and mean-spirited. Slanderous speech arises out of anger and ill will. It is always connected to anger. This form of speech breaks the harmony and friendship of community.

Harsh speech means using abusive, insulting, or sarcastic words that are spoken in anger. They are intended to cause the listener pain. Whenever anyone hears such harsh words, anger automatically arises.

Gossip and idle chatter are pointless forms of speech. There is no meaning to these words. They yield no benefit to the listener here and now in this world, or in the future after death. This form of speech fails to develop the mental qualities of the listener. Gossip gives nothing of value whatsoever in the future. It is empty. It is just talking for the sake of talking.

Not all forms of false speech are inappropriate. Suppose a teenage boy wants to go out on the town on a Friday night, but the boy's mother feels this is dangerous. The mother, who loves her son very much, says to him: "Son, please stay at home tonight because I have to go out. I need you to stay here." It is not exactly the truth that the mother is telling her son, but to prevent her son from going out and possibly getting into trouble she says: "I have to go out." This form of speech is not considered inappropriate, is not considered lying, because the words are spoken out of loving-kindness and out of compassion for her son in order to prevent him from getting into trouble. She is caring for her son.

In another story, an *arahat* and his young student live together in a forest hermitage, and the *arahat* uses the pretence of his own personal needs to create a learning situation for the student. The *arahat* uses an appropriate form of false speech to help his student realise path and fruit. This is not small talk or idle chatter.

One day the student approached the *arahat* and said: "I want to return to lay life. I am no longer interested in the life of a *bhikkhu*."

"Very well," said the *arahat*. "You are welcome to return to lay life, but the roof of your *kuṭi* is leaking and its walls are crumbling. Before you leave, will you repair the roof and walls?"

"Yes," said the student. "Before I go, I will do those repairs for you."

As the student renovated the *kuṭi*, he thought to himself: "I have only a few days here at the hermitage before I return to lay life, I might as well meditate." With his level of awareness very high, the student meditated.

After the student finished the repairs on the *kuṭi*, the *arahat* said, "My robes are dirty and are in need of washing. Will you wash them for me? I ask you to do this because after you leave I'll be living alone, and will have no one to help me."

"Yes," said the student. "I will be pleased to do that."

The student spent another day at the hermitage. He washed the *arahat*'s robes and did a few other odd jobs. Given that it was so pleasant in the newly renovated *kuṭi*, the student's mind was calm.

"You will soon leave," said the *arahat*. "Try to meditate. Try to meditate just a little bit more before you leave."

The student went to the *kuṭi* and meditated. Within a short period of time, he attained the stage of *sotāpanna*. No more doubt.

To help liberate people, the Buddha also used many different forms of speech and many different tactics. Do you remember the story of the Buddha's stepbrother Prince Nanda? The Buddha was visiting the palace of Kapilavatthu during the celebration of Nanda's engagement to the beautiful Princess Janapada Kalyāni. After the meal, the Buddha gave his bowl to his younger stepbrother and then left. Thinking that at the end of the palace grounds the Buddha would surely take his bowl back, the Prince followed his stepbrother. But at the end of the palace grounds, the Buddha did not take his bowl back and just kept on walking. Troubled, running after her Prince, Princess Kalyāni called out: "Return quickly."

Nanda had no desire to go along with the Buddha, but it was also improper to simply return to the palace. Out of respect for his older brother, Nanda felt he had to continue walking with the Buddha. With the Buddha remaining silent, the two men walked together to the park where the Buddha was staying. Finally, the Buddha took his bowl from Nanda and asked: "Will you become a *bhikkhu*?" What to do? Nanda could not refuse his older brother's wish.

"Yes," said Nanda.

Prince Nanda said he would ordain, but with a heavy heart. And after some time, it was clear that Venerable Nanda found it impossible to meditate because he was preoccupied with thoughts of his previous life at Kapilavatthu and his beautiful Princess Kalyāni. Nanda made plans to disrobe and return to lay life.

The Buddha realised this and decided to show Nanda two sights to put Nanda back on the right path. Using psychic powers, the Buddha first showed Nanda a *chena* farming area where a large tract of forested land had been cleared by burning. The whole area was burned to the ground and in the middle there was one tree standing alone, also burned. On a branch in that blackened tree clung a female monkey who had lost her ears, nose, and tail in the fire. Her body was scorched black by the fire. Venerable Nanda clearly saw this female monkey.

The second sight the Buddha showed Nanda was the Tāvatiṃsa Heaven where hundreds of pink-footed celestial nymphs waited upon Sakka, king of the *devas*. "Nanda," asked the Buddha, "which do you regard as being the more beautiful? Your noble fiancée, the Princess Janapada Kalyāni, or these celestial nymphs?"

"Venerable sir," said Nanda, "compared to these celestial nymphs, the Princess Janapada Kalyāni is like that burned moṇkey."

"I assure you Nanda," said the Buddha, "you will obtain one of these nymphs if you persevere in your meditation practice."

"In that case," said Nanda, "I shall take great pleasure in living the life of a *bhikkhu*."

The Buddha and Nanda returned to the human world, where Nanda diligently meditated with the goal of obtaining a beautiful celestial nymph. Nanda, however, quickly learned to see the true nature of phenomena. He learned to see the true nature of his craving for sensual pleasures, and he learned to let go of his craving for sensual pleasures in favour of higher and more worthwhile goals. Ultimately, he was rewarded with the fruits of the path: *arahatship*.

The words that the Buddha spoke to Prince Nanda were not lies, empty, or inappropriate. Why do you think the Buddha's words were not inappropriate?

DAVID: They were wholesome.

The Buddha's words were not inappropriate because they were based in right thought. Said out of loving-kindness and compassion for Nanda, the Buddha's words supported the development of Nanda's mental qualities. What the Buddha said to Nanda was in Nanda's best interests. Quite simply, the words were good for him.

Conversation is an area where we need to be careful. Concerning ourselves with reducing our hindrances to liberation, we speak words of truth. We speak words that bring people together, words of friendship and harmony, words that are kind and sympathetic, and words that benefit. And disregarding useless talk, we do not speak lies nor do we speak words that are slanderous, harsh, or abusive. We definitely don't gossip about others. In the Mahāsuññata Sutta of the Majjhima Nikāya you will find the topics of conversation to engage in and the topics to avoid. The commentaries have a slightly different and expanded list of topics to avoid.

I read these lists. In the list of topics to avoid, only women are mentioned and men aren't.

The Buddha was addressing a monk, Venerable Ānanda.

"When I clearly saw as it actually is with proper wisdom how sensual pleasures provide little gratification, much suffering, and much despair, and how great is the danger in them, and I attained to the rapture and pleasure that are apart from sensual pleasures, apart from unwholesome states, or to something more peaceful than that, I recognised that I was no longer attracted to sensual pleasures."

The Buddha—Cūḷadukkhakkhandha Sutta[18]

14 Right Action

Pemasiri Thera: The fourth factor of the eightfold path is right action, *sammākammanta*. With right understanding and right thought, right action means using our bodies, our physical bodies, wholesomely and appropriately:

- Respecting the rights of others to live freely
- Preserving life
- Practising generosity
- Protecting beings from harm

From cleaning our clothes and teeth to cutting our nails—there are many basic rules of appropriate conduct. For example, we know there are rules on how to properly conduct ourselves when using the toilet. If I use the toilet improperly and forget to clean it afterwards, the next person to use the toilet cannot comfortably do so. There is then a conflict between the two of us, quite possibly an argument ensues, and the harmony of our community is broken. Or say you spill a drink on the counter and make a mess. Appropriate conduct dictates that you clean up the mess. Otherwise, if you just leave the spilled drink on the counter, another person is inconvenienced because they have to take on the responsibility of cleaning up the mess. Again, a conflict arises and harmonious relations are disrupted.

Almost every day you wash the floor in our meditation hall. Conducting yourself appropriately, you are performing a good action. When meditators come to our meditation centre and see the hall is clean, they are comfortable. They like the hall and gain concentration, very easily. If the hall has not been cleaned properly, is dirty and dusty, meditators are uncomfortable. They dislike the hall and it is difficult for them to gain concentration. Keeping our meditation environment clean is important.

Rabindranath Tagore was a Nobel laureate who lived in Calcutta. On one special occasion, he was to be honored at a large tribute with tens of thousands of people in attendance. Taking place some distance from Calcutta, Tagore had to take the train to get to the tribute. As he was waiting on the platform for the train's departure, a group of men were loading soft drinks onto the train. These men, though also going to the tribute to honour Tagore, had never actually seen Tagore and didn't recognise him: "Hey! Come over here and help us."

Immediately, Tagore went over and helped the men load their cases of soft drinks onto the train. This was not a problem for Tagore. After the loading was complete, Tagore and these men boarded the train and they made their way to the tribute site. At the tribute, the men watched with embarrassment as Tagore walked onto the stage. As you see, Tagore was a humble man and, though not a Buddhist or practising Buddhism, he knew his own mind.

Right action also means abstaining from using our bodies unwholesomely and inappropriately. Everyone has the right to live freely; everyone has the right to live peacefully. To avoid disturbing another person's freedom and peace, we abstain from three types of harmful bodily actions:

1. Killing, *pānātipāta*
2. Stealing, *adinnādāna*
3. Sensual misconduct, *kāmesu micchā-cāra*

Abstaining from killing applies to any and all living beings. The life span of beings is often only a few seconds, but if we intentionally destroy those beings, that action is considered killing. We have no right to kill any being—any living being. All beings have the right to live in this world; we have no right to kill them. Even a small ant has the right to live. We have no right to take its life. Sometimes mosquitoes land on our arms and draw some blood. That is their way of living and we have no right to kill them just for doing that. We have to get away from killing. But we continue to kill.

DAVID: Is abortion killing?

Destroying, said the Buddha, what is present in the woman's body—from the time that conception has definitely taken place—is breaking the first precept. Conception means the rebirth consciousness, *paṭisandhi-viññāṇa*, arises along with the mass in the womb, linking the past *kamma* to the new *kamma*. This is conception. After the woman and the man have sex, it might be as long as two weeks before the rebirth consciousness arises.

Did they have abortion at the time of the Buddha?

Abortion is mentioned in the texts. When Queen Kosala Devi was carrying King Bimbisāra's child, it was predicted the child would grow into an adult and kill its father. Upon hearing the prediction, Queen Kosala Devi immediately tried to abort the child. But the King discouraged his Queen from doing so. As a *sotāpanna*, he neither supported nor encouraged anyone in the killing of any living being. It did not matter to King Bimbisāra that his own child was to be his deadly enemy. Queen Kosala Devi consented to her King's wishes and abstained from aborting the child. Abortion has existed throughout history. Only the methods of performing them have changed.

The second type of action we must abstain from is stealing. Everyone has the wish and the right to protect their possessions. We have no right to steal their possessions. Suppose someone steals your car. Because you need your car, you are trying to find it, may even have to buy another one. Losing possessions, looking for them, and then replacing them—such events obstruct a person's free way of living.

As human beings, we are entitled to live anywhere in this world. In the early days of civilisation, people just freely travelled from one country to another country. In those days, there were no visas and no one to issue them. People simply travelled to a country and settled down. I too can go to any country and say that I am entitled to live in that country, but they will definitely chase me out. They will say: "You have the right to live in Sri Lanka. Not here." Basically speaking, though impractical these days, as human beings we have the right to live in any country, anywhere in this world. We have the right to a free way of living. We are entitled to live peacefully.

There is nothing wrong in settling down and living in some country. What is wrong though is that after settling down, we declare: "This is my country. This is my place." What is wrong is the taking on of possession. Thus, Canadians possess their own country, Germans possess their own country, Americans possess their own country, and the English possess their own country. Everyone possesses his or her own country. We are also doing the same thing here in Sri Lanka and fighting. Possessing is unnecessary; possessing is the hindrance. Possessing leads to all the troubles. Everything arises out of possession.

The third type of action we need to abstain from is sensual misconduct. The Pali expression for abstaining from sensual misconduct is: *kāmesu micchā-cāra. Kāmesu* means craving for objects of pleasure. This word, *kāmesu*, is not in the singular form, but the plural form, which means abstinence from sensual misconduct is not only abstinence from one form of sensual misconduct. Abstaining from sensual misconduct does not only mean abstaining from physical sexual misconduct. No. Abstaining from sensual misconduct also means abstaining from abusing any of the sense doors. For example, if you use your tape recorder to listen to something inappropriate, that is also an abuse of a sense door, your ear, and falls within sensual misconduct. Or perhaps you decide to get drunk, which is an abuse of your tongue, another sense door. Using any sense door inappropriately is sensual misconduct. But today, most people only refer to sexual misconduct.

Do you mean our understanding of sense abuse in the present day?

Correct. Abuse of the senses does not only mean sexual abuse. Rape is clearly an abuse of the senses. By force you indulge in inappropriate sexual contact with another human being. You are disturbing another person's free way of living. And not only is rape an abuse. Any unsolicited sexual contact, such as molesting, is also an abuse of the senses, as it disrupts another person's freedom.

Suppose you are a married man and there is another woman who wants to have sex with you, and you want to have sex with her. If you indulge yourself with this other woman and your wife disapproves, your actions are considered an abuse of the senses. If, however, your wife approves of you having sex with the other woman, doing so is not considered an abuse of the senses. You can go and have sex with the other woman. That is the way. There has to be consensual agreement between the husband and the wife that having an extramarital affair is permissible. There has to be mutual agreement between both partners.

In ancient times, kings often had harems of one hundred or maybe even a thousand women. A contemporary of the Buddha, King Kosala had a harem and indulged in sex with any woman in his harem, at any time he wanted. Because harems were the accepted custom, no one said his behaviour was inappropriate, although he may have suffered inwardly. And even King Kosala took only two women to be his Queens: Mallikā and Vāsabhā. Most often enjoying the company of Queen Mallikā, he travelled to the Kingdom of the Sakyans with Queen Vāsabhā.

The third type of abstinence, abstaining from sensual misconduct, includes the fifth precept: abstaining from the use of intoxicants. The English wording of this precept is derived from the Pali expression: *surāmeraya-majja-pamādaṭṭhānā veramaṇī sikkhāpadaṃ samādiyāmi*, which means I undertake the training to refrain from intoxicants and drugs such as wine, liquor, etc. because they lead to carelessness. There are two words in this Pali expression that need to be discussed: *majja* and *pamāda*.

Majja means intoxicants, such as alcohol. *Majjapa* is a person who is a drunkard and has pride about his caste, education, or wealth. Activated by alcohol, his pride drives him to conduct himself inappropriately, doing many wrong things. This is *majja*.

Pamāda means negligence. The person who is negligent doesn't make the required effort to abstain from inappropriate actions or to engage in appropriate actions. They're simply lazy. Thus, they don't bother to practise compassion and loving-kindness for others or even for themselves, which disturbs everyone's free living.

Majja and *pamāda* destroy wisdom. For example, by listening to these talks and studying the *dhamma*, you are acting wisely. You are making the necessary effort to perform a wholesome action; you are doing a good deed. But when you try to fulfil some craving through your tongue by consuming alcohol, you are using your tongue foolishly. You are abusing that sense door. As a consequence of consuming alcohol, your good judgement and effort disappear, and you act inappropriately in some way. You are no longer studying the *dhamma*. Even a small measure of alcohol dulls the mind. In extreme circumstances, drunkards are led astray to murder, steal, and rape. Because a drunken person's right effort vanishes, he or she can be persuaded to engage in a variety of inappropriate actions. When right effort is absent, right mindfulness vanishes; when right mindfulness is absent, right concentration also vanishes; and without the presence of right concentration, there is no wisdom.

Over forty years ago, when I was a teenager at the Kanduboda Meditation Centre, I came to know one of Venerable Sumathipāla's relatives who was also meditating at the centre. Many years before, this man had inherited hundreds of acres of farmland and was operating a successful business. He was once very rich but he turned to drink, became a drunkard, and spent his money on drink for himself and his acquaintances. His drinking led to the mismanagement of the business and he accumulated a debt of roughly two million rupees, which was a vast sum of money at that time. To pay off this debt, he sold all but ten acres of his land. All through drink, he lost his land and his wealth.

Then he began to lose his health. Developing the disease of goitre, an enlargement of the thyroid gland, he turned for help to doctors at the hospital and to a village medicine man. The doctors recommended an operation and the medicine man tied a string around the man's swollen neck, chanted a mantra, and charged him some money. At a loss, Venerable Sumathipāla's relative didn't know what to do. He was afraid of having an operation at the hospital, and the string and the mantra did not seem to be doing much. His neck was still badly swollen. Feeling he was about to die, in desperation he went to Kanduboda to see his relative, Venerable Sumathipāla. Venerable Sumathipāla taught this man to meditate.

On one occasion, Venerable Sumathipāla left the Kanduboda Meditation Centre for six days to go on a trip. Since Venerable Sumathipāla was my teacher and I would not receive any teachings while he was away, I too left Kanduboda. I went home to visit my family. After two weeks, I returned to Kanduboda and saw Venerable Sumathipāla's relative again, but I failed to recognise him. The man I saw looked similar to Venerable Sumathipāla's relative, whom I knew quite well, but this man's neck was not swollen. Since there was no sign of goiter, I simply thought this man must be someone else and I did not even speak to him.

"Why are you ignoring me?" he asked. "Did I offend you?"

"Well," I said. "I didn't recognise you. You look different from the man I remember. Your neck is normal and your face is clear. What happened?"

"Venerable Sumathipāla is what happened," said the man. "A good operation."

The man never drank alcohol again and he supported Venerable Sumathipāla, was his *dāyakā*, up until Venerable Sumathipāla's death in 1982.

"Kassapa, when a bhikkhu develops non-enmity, non-ill-will, and a heart full of loving-kindness and, abandoning the corruptions, realises and dwells in the uncorrupted deliverance of mind, the deliverance through wisdom, having realised it in this very life by his own insight, then, Kassapa, that bhikkhu is called an ascetic and a Brahmin."

The Buddha—Mahāsīhanāda Sutta[19]

15 Right Livelihood

PEMASIRI THERA: The fifth factor of the eightfold path is right livelihood, *sammā-ājīva*. Right livelihood means:

- We earn our living by participating in wholesome and appropriate forms of livelihood, *sammā-ājīva*
- We give up any wrong forms of livelihood, *micchā-ājīva*

When we are practising right speech and practising right action, we are practising right livelihood. Keep in mind, right speech means we abstain from: (1) false speech, (2) slanderous speech, (3) harsh speech, and (4) gossip; and that right action means we abstain from: (1) killing, (2) stealing, and (3) sensual misconduct.

Countless in variety, right livelihoods are honest, peaceful, and good for the welfare of the community. In the Aṅguttara Nikāya, the Buddha names five forms of wrong livelihood, dealing in: (1) weapons, (2) living beings, (3) meat production and butchery, (4) poisons, and (5) intoxicants.

DAVID: What does the term poisons mean?

Pesticides.

Do these pesticides kill people?

Yes.

Stealing is a wrong form of livelihood. Many bosses pay their employees unfairly, and there are also many employees who work improperly. These bosses are stealing from their employees and the employees are stealing from their bosses. The actions of both parties are wrong.

Deceit and trickery are also wrong forms of livelihood. Telling fortunes, using our earlier example, is not only a wrong form of speech, but it is also a wrong form of livelihood, as fortunetellers deceive people to earn their living. Likewise, if you are a merchant who is selling dried chillies by the kilo and you add some water, you are tricking your customer. Plainly wrong.

The overcharging of people, profiteering, is another wrong form of livelihood. Suppose you buy a new tape recorder and the merchant sells it to you for 2500 rupees. It is really only worth 2000 rupees, yet he sells it to you for 2500 rupees and takes an excessive profit. That is wrong. Some people want more and more and more profit. Wanting more than a legitimate and reasonable profit, they overcharge. If you are reasonable in your business dealings with people, you are entitled to a reasonable return.

There is a good story from the time of the Buddha. A hunter killed two deer, a doe and her fawn. The hunter put the doe up for sale at, let's say, two dollars and put the fawn up for one dollar. A con man came along and bought the fawn for one dollar.

"Now," said the con man, "I gave you one dollar and you said the fawn is also worth one dollar, which adds up to two dollars. Here, I return the fawn and I'll take the doe."

The hunter accepted the fawn, gave the con man the doe, and was cheated of one dollar. Because the hunter's livelihood involved the killing of deer, it is clear that his livelihood was inappropriate. But the con man's livelihood was also inappropriate. Using deception, he cheated the hunter.

When we walk the eightfold path and truly practise *sīla*, these types of situations never arise because we are always speaking, acting, and living appropriately. At all times in our lives, we are absolutely certain of our responsibilities and committed to the wholesome. And because we are working out of compassion and loving-kindness, few conflicts arise. Life is simple and peaceful.

"Surely, Venerable Sir, we are living in concord, with mutual appreciation, without disputing, blending like milk and water, viewing each other with kindly eyes."

Venerable Anuruddha—Cūḷagosinga Sutta[20]

16 Right Effort

PEMASIRI THERA: The sixth factor of the eightfold path is right effort, *sammā-vāyāma*. It means striving for liberation from suffering. A wide-ranging topic, what the Buddha taught on right effort depended upon the listener's level of understanding, commitment, and goals. Some people were aiming at reducing suffering in their worldly lives and attaining a fortunate birth in the human or heavenly world. Hence, the Buddha taught these people how to make the appropriate effort to produce this moderate level of liberation. Others were aiming at completely overcoming all their suffering and attaining *nibbāna*. To these people, the Buddha taught ways of making the greatest of efforts and accomplishing this difficult goal—*arahatship*.

Right effort covers this whole wide range. It begins with restraint in our everyday worldly lives, through stream-entry when the canker of views is destroyed, through non-returning when the canker of craving for sensual pleasures is destroyed, and finally through to *arahatship* when the canker of craving eternal existence and the canker of ignorance are destroyed.

Mental and Physical Effort

As with so many things, mind and body interconnect in right effort. Thus, to produce wholesome actions and reduce our suffering, we must fine-tune both our mental and physical effort. When we make the right mental and physical effort, our defilements are suppressed and eventually destroyed, and we progress on the spiritual path.

Mental effort, *viriya*, means having the intention to do something. You want to practise meditation. Your reflecting over your method of meditation, whether it is *samatha* or *vipassanā*, and your intention to actually go ahead and meditate takes mental effort. In *vipassanā* meditation your intention is to note various feelings, various sounds, and various other objects, while in *samatha* meditation your intention is to keep the mind one-pointed.

Right mental effort means our intention is to restrain and abandon unwholesome actions, as well as to develop and maintain wholesome actions. We must first make the mental effort, have this mental energy within us, for wholesome verbal and bodily actions to arise. To conduct ourselves wholesomely, we must first have the intention to conduct ourselves wholesomely. Wholesome thoughts lead to wholesome actions.

When we use the term *vāyāma*, we are primarily referring to making physical, bodily effort. Clearly, your physical practice of meditation takes physical effort. Whether you are sitting or walking, you are making physical effort when you sit and walk for these forms of meditation.

Ārabhati means exerting oneself. Undertaking both mental and physical effort, we make an attempt at right effort. You, for example, are putting forth mental and also physical effort when you wash floors, rake leaves, and help with meals here at our centre. When you perform these actions without an expectation to gain something, without wanting fame or praise and simply perform these needed actions, you are performing them with right effort, with *ārabbha*. People living in community are exerting right effort when they use restraint, keep the dwellings clean, help the sick, and perform common duties.

DAVID: In early Buddhist stories, was the horse used to symbolise right effort?

Yes. A good horse is always well behaved. Even while passing urine it does so in a private place and does not, at once, just urinate anywhere. A good horse puts forth the right effort.

Ātāpī and *sampajañña* are two important Pali terms. Often united with each other, *ātāpī* means being mentally and physically enthusiastic and active, while *sampajañña* means knowing oneself, having clear comprehension, and having wisdom. Uniting the two terms, *ātāpī-sampajañña* means we make enthusiastic effort to be aware of all of our activities. In the Satipaṭṭhāna Sutta, the Buddha uses the term *ātāpī-sampajañña* to describe the quality of effort that is required to clearly comprehend the true nature of phenomena. *Ātāpī-sampajañña* is wise effort. Grounded in right understanding and right thought, it is effort that leads to right mindfulness arising. To gain *samādhi*, we must have *ātāpī-sampajañña*.

Normally, when we put effort towards performing a daily activity, we do not say we are performing that activity with *ātāpī-sampajañña*. If, however, we put our entire mental and physical effort in a completely wholesome way towards breaking free from *saṃsāra*, we are performing that activity with *ātāpī-sampajañña*. We are suffering birth, sickness, decay, death, and again birth, sickness, decay, and death. Endlessly we are suffering the unsatisfactoriness of this existence. *Ātāpī-sampajañña* means all our energy and efforts are directed towards getting away from this *saṃsāric* realm. We are striving hard.

Striving begins with our intention to constantly make four mental and physical efforts:

1. Restrain the unwholesome, *saṃvarappadhāna*
2. Abandon the unwholesome, *pahānappadhāna*
3. Develop the wholesome, *bhāvanāppadhāna*
4. Maintain the wholesome, *anurakkhaṇappadhānạ*

To understand these four efforts, we must first understand what is meant by the terms unwholesome, *akusala*, and wholesome, *kusala*.

Based in greed, aversion, and delusion, unwholesome actions by body, speech, and mind are the causes for unfavourable *kammic* results in the present and in the future. Unwholesome states include defilements, *kilesa*, and fetters, *saṃyojana*. Defilements are mind-polluting qualities, while fetters bind us to the wheel of existence. There are ten defilements and there are ten fetters, although all defilements and fetters are included in three broad categories—greed, aversion, and delusion. Unwholesome actions are the sources for all of our suffering, chain us to suffering, and perpetuate our endless wandering in *saṃsāra*.

Wholesome actions, on the other hand, include a good consciousness, good deeds, and following the eightfold path. Based in generosity, kindness, and wisdom, they are the causes for favourable *kammic* results. Wholesome actions enable us to abandon unwholesome actions. Breaking our chain to suffering, they put an end to our wandering.

Ātāpī-sampajañña is effort of the highest order. Its development involves a number of skills, attitudes, and kinds of overcoming, all of which interconnect and overlap in various ways.

Three Skills

A skill, a *kosalla*, is the proficiency in accomplishing a goal. When we think and act expertly to make progress towards accomplishing any goal, we are employing skills. As regards to making spiritual progress, we must make the effort to develop our knowledge about three skills that are listed in the Saṅgīti Sutta of the Dīgha Nikāya:

1. Skill-in-the-appropriate-way, *upāya-kosalla*
2. Skill-in-gain, *āya-kosalla*
3. Skill-in-loss, *apāya-kosalla*

Skill-in-the-Appropriate-Way

Skill-in-the-appropriate-way, *upāya-kosalla*, is the first skill. The word *upāya* means the actual ways that are available for us to accomplish our goals; *upāya* is the appropriate way to success. *Kosalla* means skill. Thus, *upāya-kosalla* means skill-in-the-appropriate-way. Skill-in-the-appropriate-way is practical cleverness. It is the knowledge about the ways to accomplish our goals, and it is the skilful employment of those ways. To progress, we must develop our knowledge about the skill-in-the-appropriate-way.

There is a Jātaka story of a small clever bird that used its practical skills, its *upāya-kosalla*, to realise a seemingly impossible goal.

The small bird lived in the jungle with three friends—a fishtail bird, a fly, and a frog. One day, a large elephant was ripping branches from trees in the small bird's area of the jungle.

"Please," said the small bird, "don't rip down this branch because you'll destroy my nest. I have done you no wrong. And like you, I am a living being who just wants to live peacefully."

"I am hungry," said the elephant. "I don't care about your nest. Besides, you are very small. How could you possibly hurt me?"

With its trunk, the elephant grabbed hold of the branch, ripped the branch off the tree, and in so doing destroyed the nest of the small bird. The small bird was very angry at the elephant and wanted to kill it. Because of the bird's small size, this seems impossible. The small clever bird went to see the fishtail bird.

"You are my friend," said the small bird. "I need your help."

"For what?" asked the fishtail bird.

"An elephant intentionally destroyed my nest and I want revenge. I need you to peck its eyes." The fishtail bird agreed, found the elephant, and pecked its eyes. The small bird went next to the fly.

"Fly," said the small bird. "I need your help. Please go to this mean elephant and lay eggs in its damaged eyes." The fly found the elephant, laid eggs in the elephant's eyes and, as the maggots grew, the elephant's condition became worse and worse. Eventually, the elephant went completely blind. The bird went to visit the frog.

"Friend," said the bird. "I need your help because an elephant intentionally destroyed my nest and I want to punish it. I want to kill this elephant. With the help of fishtail bird and fly, it is now blind and must use its sense of hearing to find water. With your croaking sounds, will you lead him to the top of that high mountain?"

"Yes," said the frog. "I will do that for you."

The frog found the elephant. And desperate for water, the blind elephant walked towards the frog's croaking sounds. All the way to the top of the mountain, the elephant followed the frog's croaks. When the frog finally had the elephant at the edge of a high cliff, the frog croaked one last time as it jumped safely to one side. The elephant could not see where it was going and when it walked towards the sound of the frog's croak, the elephant fell off the cliff, crashed to the ground below, and died a terrible and painful death.

The small bird had the skill and ability to destroy that huge elephant. It used its *upāya-kosalla*.

The bird's actions weren't very wholesome.

The story is just an example to give some meaning to the term *upāya-kosalla*. Despite its small size, the bird achieved an apparently impossible goal: destruction of the elephant. The small bird could do this because it used its skill-in-the-appropriate-way; the bird worked skilfully according to existing circumstances. And just as the small bird made effort and employed skilful ways to destroy the huge elephant, we need to employ all of our skill-in-the-appropriate-way to destroy our own elephant, to destroy our huge burden of unwholesomeness. This is accomplished by making the right effort.

When we are mindful, when we clearly comprehend the true nature of phenomena, and when we implement wisdom to destroy unwholesome actions, we are using *upāya-kosalla*. Little by little with *ātāpī-sampajañña*—with wise mental and physical effort—we use our knowledge about the skill-in-the-appropriate-way to distance ourselves from unwholesome things, reduce the hindrances to a wholesome mind, and develop the factors that promote a wholesome mind.

You said the small bird's actions were unwholesome. I told you this story just to demonstrate the potential of acting skilfully. Skill-in-the-appropriate-way, however, is always associated with wholesome thinking and the performance of wholesome actions, and is never associated with the unwholesome. We have to put our knowledge about the skill-in-the-appropriate-way towards the good of other beings and ourselves, and not towards killing, harming people, or anything like that.

By putting the appropriate skills into our practice, we do away with the obstacles in our way, destroy our unwholesome states and actions, and make progress on the path. When we use our skill-in-the-appropriate-way, we achieve our goals. For example, I cannot easily climb a tree, but I can climb a tree when I use a ladder. I am using my *upāya-kosalla*. And my using a ladder to climb a tree is no different from using skills to progress along the spiritual path.

We make use of right effort to progress, use *ātāpī-sampajañña*. There are many people in our community who are making the necessary mental and physical effort, are practising meditation, and are getting away from unwholesome things. They are trying hard. They have some skill-in-the-appropriate-way, *upāya-kosalla*, and are striving for *nibbāna*, but they need the supporting powers.

For people to develop their mental qualities and meditation practice, the most important supporting power is their fellow human beings. This is very important because meditators, even when they have some knowledge about the skill-in-the-appropriate-way, simply cannot practise properly unless the fellow members of their community also have some knowledge about the skill-in-the-appropriate-way. On their own, meditators cannot practise. To practise properly, the meditator must be compatible with fellow members of their meditation community, and all members of the community must be working together to achieve the same goal. A supportive community is very important. It is the key to success.

A community that is not supportive is an obstruction to the practice. For example, some people living in meditation centres speak and act in ways that are inappropriate for meditation centres. Because they have not established right understanding within themselves, they do not have the intention to exert the right mental and physical effort. These people are lacking in knowledge about skill-in-the-appropriate-way, which weakens our mental and physical effort.

We have chosen to have these *dhamma* discussions at 5:00 a.m. because it is a quiet time of the day and there are fewer obstructions to learning. But when someone nearby turns on his radio, unpleasant feelings arise and our *dhamma* discussions are disrupted. "Why," we ask, "is this man playing his radio while we are trying to learn the *dhamma*?" His actions are disruptive and undermine our efforts.

Suppose we start these *dhamma* discussions at midnight because we think there is less likelihood of anyone disturbing us at that time. But when someone discovers we are still awake, they will make us a cup of tea. It is okay. They can make us some tea, but the point is that they are unaware that we are trying to learn the *dhamma*, and they are unaware that we are trying to make some progress towards liberation. Instead of being sensitive and supporting that process, they make idle conversation, make noise while they prepare the tea, and disturb our free way of flowing. They completely ignore what is going on in our *dhamma* discussion. A person who behaves in this way has no *upāya-kosalla*.

At all times in our lives, we need knowledge about the skill-in-the-appropriate-way, *upāya-kosalla*. We need *upāya-kosalla* to solve our day-to-day problems, and we need *upāya-kosalla* to know how to conduct ourselves with this and that person in this and that circumstance. We need knowledge about the skill-in-the-appropriate-way to see situations clearly and to work with wisdom according to what is required. In this world, we must employ some knowledge and wisdom.

Skill-in-the-appropriate-way. We train in the skill of knowing our weaknesses and we train in the skill of overcoming our weaknesses. We make some effort.

Am I practising skill-in-the-appropriate-way when I know that I am angry?

Yes. Knowing you are angry and knowing how to overcome your anger is skill-in-the-appropriate-way.

Is it enough to know that I am angry?

No. Just knowing that your unwholesome state is present is insufficient. You also need to develop the skill in overcoming your anger. The knowledge is in knowing these skills and the wisdom is in knowing that you must develop them. This is the nature of right understanding. When we have right understanding, we really know that we have no choice but to make the effort to conduct ourselves appropriately.

You wash floors and rake leaves at this centre. Now it is unnecessary for you to do this work, but you do it. If while working you are abandoning your unwholesome states and developing your wholesome states, you are working in the right spirit: with *upāya-kosalla.* Wholesomeness requires cultivation. Generosity, for example, requires being generous. We do not simply carry the view that we are generous. No. We perform kind actions. We help people.

I sometimes give money to beggars, but I am often overwhelmed by their aggressiveness.

You have to use *upāya-kosalla* when associating with beggars. Many years ago when I first considered ordaining, I lived with beggars to determine whether I was fit to lead the life of a *bhikkhu.* I lived with them on the street and in their shacks, and I ate whatever they ate. In so doing, I discovered many interesting things about their ways. I remember one beggar who used to get a lot of money from begging. But when he felt hungry, he just left most of his money on the pavement and went off to the store to buy some bread. Even though this man was a beggar, he wasn't greedy.

Some beggars are quite reasonable.

There are two kinds of beggars: one is genuine and the other is a fraud. The genuine beggar begs only once a day and is satisfied with whatever he receives. When a genuine beggar says he wants food, he only wants food; and when a genuine beggar says he wants clothes, he only wants clothes. A genuine beggar never asks for anything more beyond this. When you tell a genuine beggar that this amount of money is all you want to give, he simply accepts that amount of money. He never complains that you haven't given enough.

In contrast, the fraud begs again and again in the course of the same day and is never satisfied. This person is just collecting things. When you tell the fraud that this amount of money is all you want to give, he doesn't simply accept your gift. When he feels you should give more, he asks for more. And if you do not give more, he complains. He is never satisfied. This is the difference between a genuine beggar and a fraud.

The Buddha mentioned various types of beggars who were dependent upon the generosity of others: *samaṇas*, *brāhmaṇas*, *vaṇibbakas*, *kapaṇas*, and those called *pulanno* in Sinhalese. The *samaṇas* and the *brāhmaṇas* were the wandering ascetics, the religious recluses, and those leading a pure life. *Vaṇibbakas* praised potential donors with kind words. "Good gentleman," they said, or "Good lady," and then they begged. The *kapaṇas* were destitute, in great need and just asked for assistance. They simply begged. And the *pulanno* were also in great need, were hungry and improperly clothed, but they did not beg, although they expected someone to help. They still had that expectation. But they never directly asked anyone for help because they felt ashamed. They remained silent.

Though we do not have any entirely genuine beggars in Sri Lanka these days, there are many people who are in real need and it is a wholesome action to help them. It is a particularly wholesome action to assist those who are in need, but aren't asking for help. We have to put our generosity into the practice, and if we have the skill-in-the-appropriate-way, we recognise which man or woman is genuine, which one is a fraud, and we know how to help in each case.

I am angry at one particular *bhikkhu* because he complains about the food in a poor neighbourhood. I dislike that he is ungrateful for the alms he is given. How do I use *upāya-kosalla*?

I know this young *bhikkhu* and he related the same story to me. His English is poor and it is difficult for him to express himself clearly to you. What he told me was that he went on alms round to this destitute and dirty neighbourhood out of compassion for these people. *Bhikkhus* rarely go on alms round to this neighbourhood because the people living there are dirty, the surroundings are dirty, and even the food is dirty. This *bhikkhu* thought that he must go to this poor neighbourhood for these very reasons.

This isn't the answer I am looking for.

Making the effort to understand how this *bhikkhu* really went to the people in that neighbourhood is using your *upāya-kosalla*. You misunderstood this *bhikkhu* because he doesn't speak English very well. He made up his mind to intentionally go to these unpleasant places and in so doing revealed his skilful effort and compassion. In his actions, there was a lot of *upāya-kosalla*. Now you know why he went.

I also used to go on alms round to similar neighbourhoods. Among the Sinhalese there are snake charmers and others who are regarded as low caste. They are extremely dirty. I used to go to their homes and receive their offerings of food. The unclean manner in which this food was prepared and the way it tasted made it difficult to eat, and for two days after receiving this food my alms bowl smelled bad. The food they offered me was very dirty, but I ate it because of the Buddha *Sāsana*. I went to the homes of these poor people, accepted and ate their food, because the Buddha advised his *bhikkhus* to do this out of compassion and for their own development. I followed the Buddha's advice and as a result my *viriya*, my mental effort and energy, developed and increased.

My wealthy supporters in Colombo scolded me for going to those poor neighbourhoods. If I go on alms round to these wealthy supporters' homes, there are no problems, difficulties, or challenges for me. They receive me with the highest honour and give me the finest food. There is no problem at all. But going to the homes of these poor people who can only offer leftovers, scraps of odds and ends, is more of a challenge. In his previous existences, the Buddha went on alms round to poor and unclean neighbourhoods. That was *upāya-kosalla*. This young *bhikkhu* went to these poor neighbourhoods with the same purpose in mind. He went out of compassion.

Okay. Thank you.

Wholesome strengths and knowledge about the skill-in-the-appropriate-way are not innate. We must develop and train in them. When we develop our strengths and skills, our wholesomeness develops and grows stronger. We overcome our weaknesses and progress on the path.

Am I developing my strengths when I know I am doing something right?

Yes. Make the effort to know your strengths, but remember to know your weaknesses. When we know our strengths as well as our weaknesses, we develop and maintain our strengths, and we suppress and overcome our weaknesses. We need to develop the proper ways of knowing the gain of these wholesome strengths, and we also need to develop the proper ways of knowing the loss of our unwholesome weaknesses. We develop understanding of whatever occurs in our lives, and eventually we come to a stage where it is unnecessary to develop wholesome strengths: wholesomeness is purely present.

I'm not at that stage.

Good. At least you know that much.

Skill-in-Gain

Skill-in-gain, *āya-kosalla,* is the second skill listed in the Sangīti Sutta. *Āya* means we are making progress, going forward towards our goal, and making real gains. This term, skill-in-gain, means that the man or woman has entered the stream to *nibbāna* and is free from the first three of the ten fetters:

1. Personality view, *sakkāya-diṭṭhi*
2. Sceptical doubt, *vicikicchā*
3. Clinging to mere rules and rituals, *Sīlabbata-parāmāsa*

Knowledge about the skill-in-gain, *āya-kosalla*, is a significant improvement. Getting away from these three fetters is a major gain.

Does *āya-kosalla* mean the person is a *sotāpanna*?

Yes. Knowledge about the skill-in-gain, *āya-kosalla*, means you know the wholesomeness that is present in you and you know that you must develop this wholesomeness even further. *Āya-kosalla* means you have accomplished stream-entry and to a certain degree you have completed your work—you have destroyed three of your fetters and have become a *sotāpanna*. Your work from that point onwards is to destroy the seven remaining fetters and become an *arahat*. With the attainment of skill-in-gain, you would have that wholesome strength and ability.

Skill-in-Loss

Skill-in-loss, *apāya-kosalla*, is the third skill. This term *apāya* is generally associated with the four lower worlds—animal, ghost, demon, and hell. But in the context of skills, the term *apāya* means loss. *Apāya* means the man or woman has lost all ten fetters. In addition to losing the first three fetters, they have lost the remaining seven:

4. Sensual pleasure passion, *kāma-rāga*
5. Ill will, *vyāpāda*
6. Fine-material passion, *rūpa-rāga*
7. Immaterial passion, *arūpa-rāga*
8. Conceit, *māna*
9. Restlessness, *uddhacca*
10. Ignorance, *avijjā*

Knowledge about the skill-in-loss is a complete loss of all ten fetters, destruction of all unwholesomeness. It means the man or woman is enlightened. He or she is an *arahat*.

Is skill-in-gain the first step towards enlightenment and skill-in-loss the second step?

Knowledge about the skill-in-gain, *āya-kosalla*, means freedom from the first three of the ten fetters, becoming a *sotāpanna*; knowledge about the skill-in-loss, *apāya-kosalla*, means freedom from the seven remaining fetters, becoming an *arahat*; and knowledge about the skill-in-the-appropriate-way, *upāya-kosalla*, refers to the whole process.

Are the three skills connected?

Yes. Little by little, we proceed by making use of our knowledge about the skill-in-the-appropriate-way. As beings tied to the wheel of existence, we're still developing what has to be developed and we're abandoning what has to be abandoned. Therefore, dependent upon our relative degree of right understanding, we act as skilfully as possible to develop wholesomeness and abandon unwholesomeness. At any time in any situation, we act as wisely as possible. We develop the skill to know how to act in the moment. When situations arise that are hindrances to our *samādhi*, we know how to deal with those particular hindrances and maintain our *samādhi*. This is not easy. But by diligently putting as much skill-in-the-appropriate-way into the practice as we have at our disposal, we gradually proceed until our knowledge about skill-in-gain matures and bears its fruit—freedom from the first three fetters.

Sotāpanna is reached at this stage and we have entered the stream that flows towards *arahatship*. Still, we must continue to work hard to develop the wholesome and abandon the unwholesome until our knowledge about skill-in-loss matures and bears its fruit—freedom from the seven remaining fetters. At this highest stage of attainment, *arahatship* is reached and it is now neither necessary to develop wholesome strengths and qualities, nor is it necessary to abandon unwholesome weaknesses. At this stage, you simply have no unwholesomeness. You are finished. Knowledge about the skill-in-loss, *apāya-kosalla*, is the highest point of right understanding.

Developing *apāya-kosalla* is dependent upon the attainment of *āya-kosalla*; otherwise, you cannot proceed to *apāya-kosalla*. And this whole process is collectively called knowledge about the skill-in-the-appropriate-way, *upāya-kosalla*. Knowledge about the skill-in-the-appropriate-way is the cause that leads to the effect of attaining enlightenment, in finally becoming an *arahat*. That is the effect.

We have many stories from the Buddha's time of people who lived a good lay life, developed the appropriate skills, and walked towards *nibbāna*. Typically, we refer to the life of the millionaire Sudatta. He was exceptionally generous and as a result became known as Anāthapiṇḍika, feeder of the helpless. Anāthapiṇḍika developed generosity to a very high level and at an early age attained to stream-entry.

Didn't he build the Jētavana Monastery?

Yes. To support the Buddha and the *saṅgha*, Anāthapiṇḍika built Jētavana. There was a park in Sāvatthi district that was owned by Prince Jēta. Wishing to build the monastery in this park, Anāthapiṇḍika asked Prince Jēta if he could buy it.

"No. It's not for sale," said the Prince.

But Anāthapiṇḍika's wish to buy the park was great. In an effort to persuade the Prince to change his mind, Anāthapiṇḍika intended to cover the grounds of the park with gold coins. Before he was able, however, to totally cover the park grounds with gold, Anāthapiṇḍika went bankrupt and had to leave a small piece of the grounds uncovered. When Prince Jēta saw what Anāthapiṇḍika had done, he was inspired by the strength of Anāthapiṇḍika's wish to buy the park. Not only did the Prince agree to sell, but he went one step farther and donated the piece of land that Anāthapiṇḍika was unable to cover.

Anāthapiṇḍika had knowledge about the skill-in-the-appropriate-way and knowledge about the skill-in-gain. He had enough right understanding and right thought to give him the confidence to make the necessary effort. He really walked the spiritual path.

The *bodhisatta* Siddhārtha Gautama also used *upāya-kosalla* in his search for enlightenment. From ascetics of different sects, he accepted ways that benefited his search and he declined ways that hindered his search. Near the end of his search, Siddhārtha associated with only seven people: two meditation teachers and five ascetics. His two meditation teachers, Ālāra Kalāma and Uddaka Rāmaputta, were father and son. The *bodhisatta* Siddhārtha developed his knowledge about all three skills—skill-in-the-appropriate-way, skill-in-gain, skill-in-loss—and attained enlightenment. The Buddha discusses knowledge of these three skills in the Mahāsīhanāda Sutta in the Dīgha Nikāya.

Are you following?

I think so. Does the *arahat* cultivate wholesomeness?

No. Once you reach the stage of *arahat*, you know it is unnecessary to intentionally cultivate wholesome actions as a way to liberation because you are free from unwholesome actions. You know you are a pure being, know you are liberated, and consequently you act wholesomely. The *arahat* walked the noble eightfold path, abandoned what had to be abandoned, developed what had to be developed, and attained to the final stage of liberation. An *arahat* has come to the end of his or her journey.

Ultimately, we too must let go of our craving to develop wholesomeness as well as let go of our craving to abandon unwholesomeness because our craving for these spiritual gains obstructs the development of wisdom. The *dhamma* is a raft we use to cross over the dangerous river of *saṃsāra*. When we get to the other side, we don't carry the raft on our heads.

Three Attitudes

An elementary attitude is the attitude required for progress. The term elementary means elements in the sense of the simplest component parts of any whole. Elements, *dhātu* in Pali, are the primary, rudimentary, and basic constituents of larger units. In all material phenomena, for example, there are four great primary elements—earth, fire, water, and wind. With respect to attitudes of the path, the term elementary means the basic ways of appropriate thinking, the first principles, which are required for liberation from suffering. There are three elementary attitudes:

1. Inception-elementary-attitude, *ārambha-dhātu*
2. Renunciation-elementary-attitude, *nekkhamma-dhātu*
3. Courageous-striving-elementary-attitude, *parakkama-dhātu*

These three elementary attitudes are phases of mental energy through which we pass to attain liberation. The first elementary attitude is inception, *ārambha-dhātu*. Inception is the beginning of an action. With regard to spiritual progress, inception-elementary-attitude means we realise that we need to develop spiritually. It occurs to us that we have to abandon our unwholesome ways and develop more wholesome ways. Thus, we make the initial effort to do so. We take on regular exercises such as intending to perform wholesome actions and we actually begin to perform some wholesome actions, all with the plan to attain *nibbāna*. There is a beginning of taking on this work and from that point onwards we have entered upon the path.

Some people do no more than begin to take on the work. That is all. They start to understand and recognise their unwholesomeness. But despite this degree of insight into their nature, they have no energy to abandon their unwholesomeness, and again fall into their same old ways. Unwholesome things drag them down. With the arising of the inception-elementary-attitude, these people start to understand and recognise their unwholesome ways and truly have some knowledge about the skill-in-the-appropriate-way, *upāya-kosalla*, but they have no energy to go forward and as a result do various other things. But they start with that inception-elementary-attitude. They start with that basic initial intention to attain *nibbāna*, but from there on—nothing.

Do these people like their unwholesomeness?

No. They just don't have the energy to abandon it.

Does abandoning take more energy than they have?

True. They need more energy, need to make a greater mental effort, but they do not have the energy to make the necessary effort. And their path leads another way, away from *nibbāna*. They stop meditating and switch onto various other activities. It could be that when they got on this path they only imagined they were letting go of their attachments—spouse, children, property. But in fact,they were and are still holding onto these things, which is why they have no energy to go forward. To move towards *nibbāna*, we need the inception-elementary-attitude, *ārambha-dhātu*. Start with that attitude.

The second elementary attitude is renunciation, *nekkhamma-dhātu*. Renunciation means we have recognised and understood our unwholesomeness —our greed, aversion, delusion—and abandoned it, let it go. We reject unwholesome things and are proceeding forward. Even while living a lay life with a spouse and children, an attitude of renunciation can be adopted. At the same time that household duties are being properly performed, unwholesomeness is abandoned and wholesomeness is developed. We drop our attachment to our unwholesome ways. Renunciation-elementary-attitude means walking on the path.

Is a person who has an attitude of renunciation a *sotāpanna*?

We must not meditate to become a *sotāpanna* nor to gain the first mental absorption. Our intention must always be towards *nibbāna.* Suppose you are working for that goal and on the way you find you become a *sotāpanna.* That is fine. There is nothing wrong with that. You are carrying a basket of ten eggs when someone bumps into you and three of your ten eggs break. It is an accident. Likewise, you are working towards *arahatship* and on the way you happen to destroy the first three fetters; you become a *sotāpanna.* We must have the intention to destroy all ten fetters. That is real effort—real *vāyāma* and real *viriya.*

If we realise the renunciation-elementary-attitude, we are like the small but clever bird: we blind the elephant.

The third elementary attitude is courageous striving, *parakkama-dhātu.* Courageous striving means we are seeking for truth with as much effort and as bravely as we possibly can. This is the ultimate attitude. This is the attitude we need to make the final effort, to put forth the highest possible energy, to attain our goal, and become an *arahat.* Through this attitude of courageous striving, we make the effort to overcome obstacles and experience peace. Achieving some success in our practice, we are encouraged to further exert ourselves. More effort yields more positive results. Advancing in this way, we continue to progress until we reach *nibbāna.* We destroy the elephant.

Three Kinds of Overcoming

Once a degree of wisdom, right understanding and right thought, is established, we make the effort to overcome unwholesomeness. We rise above our laziness.

There are three kinds of overcoming:

1. Overcoming-by-opposites, *tadaṅga-pahāna*
2. Overcoming-by-suppression, *vikkhambhana-pahāna*
3. Overcoming-by-destruction, *samuccheda-pahāna*

The three kinds of overcoming correspond to the three divisions of the eightfold path: *sīla*, *samādhi*, and *paññā.*

In the beginning, we have enough wisdom to distinguish between the wholesome and the unwholesome. We follow the precepts, speak and act properly, and obey society's rules. There is a commitment to the wholesome. Because of ignorance, however, the tendency to crave and thus perform unwholesome actions, such as speaking and acting improperly, still crops up. But we restrain ourselves. We overcome our unwholesome actions with their opposites, which are wholesome actions. We apply overcoming-by-opposites.

As our wisdom develops, we recognise the need to go beyond overcoming-by-opposites because we find our tendency to crave and perform unwholesome actions disturbing. Through concentration, through *samādhi*, we suppress our tendency to crave and perform unwholesome actions. We suppress the five hindrances. Without support of the hindrances, no unwholesome actions are performed and no unwholesome effects arise. Nonetheless, despite applying overcoming-by-suppression, unwholesomeness still lies buried below the surface. How far it is buried depends upon the strength of our *samādhi*.

To dig unwholesomeness up by its roots, we must develop our wisdom, our *paññā*, through the practice of *vipassanā* meditation. When our *vipassanā* is strong, we see that all sense objects continually arise and pass away, arise and pass away. Penetrating the true nature of sense objects—impermanent, unsatisfactory, and insubstantial—we attain path knowledge. The *paññā* of path knowledge is overcoming-by-destruction, the final kind of overcoming. Unwholesomeness is destroyed.

Sīla, *samādhi*, and *paññā*. Overcoming-by-opposites, overcoming-by-suppression, and overcoming-by-destruction—the three kinds of overcoming develop gradually. Wisely employing our knowledge about the skill-in-the-appropriate-way, we overcome unwholesomeness by its opposite and by its suppression. With more effort, we overcome more unwholesomeness. This is the way.

Eventually, our skill in overcoming unwholesomeness develops to the point of destroying some unwholesomeness. Free from the first three of our ten fetters, we become *sotāpannas*, and have knowledge about the skill-in-gain, *āya-kosalla*. At the stage of *sotāpanna*, we completely destroy some unwholesomeness, although not all unwholesomeness. We still have seven fetters binding us in *saṃsāra*.

To abandon the seven remaining fetters, we practise additional overcoming-by-opposites, practise additional overcoming-by-suppression, gain more insights, and further develop our wisdom. Repeatedly. Constantly, we continue to practise overcoming-by-opposites; repeatedly and constantly, we practise overcoming-by-suppression; and we gradually move farther and farther away from our fetters. Again and again, more overcoming-by-opposites and more overcoming-by-suppression until, finally, we completely destroy all ten of our fetters, and become *arahats*. And that is knowledge about the skill-in-loss, *apāya-kosalla*.

In the practice of meditative development, effort must be balanced and right, and that means it must have its foundation in right understanding and right thought. When phenomena are seen clearly, right effort naturally arises.

Without a foundation in right understanding and right thought, effort is unbalanced and produces suffering. For example, unbalanced effort generates fixed views, *micchā-diṭṭhi*: good deeds must be performed, white clothes must always be worn when practising meditation, one's own way is correct and others' ways are wrong. We find many meditators like this. Always seeing others from their own point of view, they think they are correct and all others are wrong. Out of an unbalanced effort, they have developed fixed views.

Unbalanced effort also leads people to use extreme methods such as self-torture, the *atta-kilamatha* method, or its opposite, *kāma-sukha*, which is the overindulgence in sensual pleasures. If you are practising self-torture, you use painful methods such as fasting and sleep deprivation to restrain and abandon your unwholesomeness. You are trying to break your attachment to sensual pleasures through denial and torment. You go for long periods of time without washing your body or taking care of yourself properly. This is effort that has gone to the extremely painful, self-torture side. Yes, the person who practises self-torture is making mental and physical effort. But the elementary attitudes of inception, renunciation, and courageous striving do not apply because this type of practice is not leading completely towards *nibbāna*. Because meditators are trying to find liberation from a wrong way, they continue to suffer.

Overindulgence in sensual pleasures is the opposite extreme of self-torture. Indulgence certainly does give a degree of pleasure, but this pleasure is coarse, short-lived, and unsatisfactory.

Neither self-torture nor overindulging in sensual pleasures lead to the end of suffering. In fact, these two forms of effort are actually increasing instead of decreasing suffering. "These two extremes," the Buddha stated, "are useless and profitless, and must be abandoned." However, the Buddha did recommend that it was better to practise self-torture than to overindulge in sensual pleasures.

In the Buddha's first discourse, recorded in the Dhammacakkappavattana Sutta of the Saṃyutta Nikāya, the middle path was explained. The middle path is the noble eightfold path. It lies between the path of self-torture and the path of overindulging in sensual pleasures. Only the middle path decreases suffering and leads to the end of suffering.

Right effort is the heart of the middle path, the eightfold path. It means having the right understanding of phenomena, and it means having the right thought to attain liberation. Constantly making mental and physical effort, we restrain and abandon the unwholesome, and we develop and maintain the wholesome. Working hard, we make the effort to develop the attitudes and skills necessary to attain freedom from unwholesomeness.

We start with the inception-elementary-attitude and gain knowledge about the skill-in-the-appropriate-way. We proceed with the renunciation-elementary-attitude and knowledge about the skill-in-gain until, with the courageous-striving-elementary-attitude, we gain knowledge about skill-in-loss and arrive at the end of our journey—*nibbāna*.

Mental and physical effort, attitudes, kinds of overcoming, and a variety of skills—many different elements come together in right effort.

Siddhārtha made the right effort. He first had the intention to become a *buddha* and then strove with diligence, *appamāda*, to attain that goal. He made the effort to practise meditation with various teachers, to practise meditation on his own, to surmount his obstacles, and to fully develop an attitude of renunciation. With knowledge about the skill-in-the-appropriate-way and knowledge about the skill-in-gain developed, Siddhārtha's attitude eventually became one of courageous striving and he made the crucial effort, the highest possible effort, to develop knowledge about skill-in-loss and he attained liberation—Siddhārtha became the Buddha.

We also must strive with diligence. Maintaining the necessary mental and physical effort, we conduct ourselves appropriately, develop proper concentration, and increase our wisdom. Diligence is the strong stem that connects us to wisdom. The stem that connects a mango to its tree may be small, but it doesn't break because it is extremely strong. When we are really and truly diligent, we connect to wisdom and attain *arahatship*.

Negligence, *pamāda*, is the opposite of diligence. Apathetic and lazy, a man or woman stops making the necessary effort required to conduct him or herself appropriately, stops making the effort to perform wholesome actions.

Negligence means right effort is absent. When right effort is absent, right mindfulness never arises. Without the arising of right mindfulness, there is never any arising of right concentration. And without right concentration, there is no wisdom.

Of all the fragrant flowers in Sri Lanka, the jasmine is considered the most fragrant. Of all the fragrant roots in Sri Lanka, once again only one is considered the most fragrant—the root of the *kalu-agil* tree. And just as the fragrances of jasmine and the root of the *kalu-agil* tree stand out above all other fragrances, diligence stands out above all other wholesome qualities. Diligence must be the dominant aspect of our lives. With diligence, we exert right effort, develop our wisdom, make progress, and achieve liberation.

"This is the direct path for the purification of beings, for the surmounting of sorrow and lamentation, for the disappearance of pain and grief, for the attainment of the true way, for the realisation of nibbāna namely, the four foundations of mindfulness."

The Buddha—Satipaṭṭhāna Sutta[21]

17 Right Mindfulness

PEMASIRI THERA: The seventh factor of the eightfold path is right mindfulness, *sammā-sati*. *Sati* is the Pali term for a wholesome, *kusala*, state of mind. It is the mind-state that is inseparably linked with wholesomeness, not mixed up with or touched by anything harmful. When we perform wholesome actions, *sati* is present. It is present when we are generous and present when we are kind. It is present when we maintain a meditation centre, when we observe the five or eight precepts, and we follow the eightfold path.

"All wholesome states of mind," said the Buddha in the Aṅguttara Nikāya, "are *sati*." All.

Acts of generosity performed without expectations are acts being performed with *sati*. When we help people without expectation, we are helping them with *sati*. When you clean the floor in the meditation hall without any expectations, you are cleaning with *sati*. And when you perform any virtuous deed without expectation, you are performing it with *sati*. *Sati* is observing the five and eight precepts without expectation and it is following the eightfold path, without expectation.

Actions performed with expectations are not being performed with *sati*. Acts of generosity in which there is an expectation of future becoming in a good plane, of praise, of fame, or of obtaining anything at all are not completely wholesome acts of generosity and thus are not being performed with *sati*. Generally, any act of generosity is a wholesome act, but at the point where expectations are present, there is no *sati*. In the same way, if we are observing precepts with the expectation to get to an eternal plane or to gain favourable future results, our state of mind has not reached the level of *sati*; our minds are mixed up with ignorance at that point. Even though making the effort to observe the precepts is a beneficial state of mind, there is no *sati* at the point where expectations are present.

The concept of a wholesome state of mind existed before Siddhārtha became the enlightened Buddha: people kept precepts and they practised generosity, kindness, and compassion. There already existed a tradition of developing a wholesome state of mind and this mind-state was called *sati*. People practised *sati* in an effort to attain favourable results, such as a birth in a permanent place where they would live in peace for all eternity. They did not practise *sati* to achieve anything beyond these types of results.

Siddhārtha realised that practising *sati* in this way only led to decay and death, only perpetuated endless suffering in *saṃsāra*, and set out on a quest to find a more satisfactory form of liberation. Eventually, Siddhārtha discovered that overcoming decay and death required turning the body, activities performed with the body, experiences of the body and the mind, and all the thoughts of the mind completely towards the wholesome and skilful. Training his body and mind in this way, Siddhārtha attained enlightenment and became the Buddha, subsequently teaching liberating truths to all who wanted to listen. As a result of these teachings, the goal of practising *sati* changed from attaining conditioned results that are subject to decay and death, to one of going beyond decay and death and attaining the unconditioned—*nibbāna*. The Buddha called this way of practice the noble, *ariyan sati*, *sammā-sati*.

Through the practice of *sati*, we break free of *saṃsāra*. *Sati* means we have no expectations whatsoever. There is only the thought that our existence in *saṃsāra* is *dukkha* and that there is decay and death here. Just to get beyond that, to overcome that, is the only thought in our minds. That is *sati*. Just that one thought in mind, that all we are looking for is to go beyond *saṃsāra*, to go beyond decay and death.

Attention

Paying attention, *manasikāra*, is similar to *sati*: a mindful awareness is present. Attention, however, is only the faculty of our minds to observe phenomena. It is nothing more than this faculty of observance. Through paying attention, we turn our minds towards objects of experience.

Picture a room. There are many people in the room and a guard stands at its entrance. The guard's duty is to open and close the door to the room, and that is all. He does nothing else. The guard never goes wandering around and talking with the people inside the room, and he never goes wandering around outside the room. No. The guard just remains at the entrance to the room, opening and closing the door. This room is our mind, the people in the room are the factors of our mind, and the guard who opens and closes the door is our faculty of attention.

By using our faculty of attention, we turn our minds towards objects of experience. Paying attention is nothing more than turning our minds towards a variety of different objects. It is a neutral faculty that supports the performance of wholesome actions, neutral actions, and unwholesome actions. This is the nature of beings. An eel has a head like a snake and a tail like a fish. When an eel sees a snake, it turns its head towards the snake; when an eel sees a fish, it turns its tail towards the fish. *Manasikāra* is an eel. Sometimes it turns towards wholesomeness and sometimes it turns towards unwholesomeness.

DAVID: The cliché is that of a skilled thief.

Yes. When a thief breaks into a house, he uses his faculty of attention, *manasikāra*. He is very aware of walking, speaking, and all movements. Maybe he breaks in through the roof. If a thief makes a mistake and gets caught, we say: "Hey. You have no *sati*." But it is wrong to say this because actions performed with *sati* are free of expectations and of course a thief expects to gain something. Therefore, his form of attention is not *sati*. Having no expectations whatsoever, even when performing good actions, is the cause for attaining *nibbāna*.

'No expectations' is the cause for *nibbāna*—that's radical.

When people who are new to meditation forget something, we also say: "Hey. You have no *sati*." We say this in order to develop their mindfulness, but after a while we have to explain to them what is *sati* and what is just paying attention, *manasikāra*. But to help meditators who are just starting to develop a practice, we say: "You have no *sati*."

Right now, I am doing many different things and I place my eyeglasses on the table. After our discussion, I will get up and go somewhere. There's a chance I will forget that just now I placed my eyeglasses on the table.

"Pemasiri," some people might say, "has no *sati*. That teacher has no mindfulness." But these people are wrong to say that because my forgetfulness is not a lapse in *sati*. It's true, I may be paying little attention to where I place my eyeglasses, but I am still carrying on with my *sati*, my wholesome state of mind. That is all that is happening. Many people think forgetfulness is a lapse in *sati*. We can't say that.

Even while practising *sati* correctly, a very good meditator sometimes forgets things—he can have a bath at the well and forget his bar of soap or he can brush his teeth and forget his toothbrush. The meditator forgets the bar of soap or the toothbrush because he is not turning his attention, his *manasikāra*, towards the bar of soap or towards the toothbrush. Instead, at that particular moment in time the meditator is turning his attention towards some other object of experience, such as his mind. The meditator is simply not turning his faculty of attention towards the bar of soap or the toothbrush, and as a result forgets them.

Paying attention, *manasikāra*, is merely the faculty of being aware of an object of experience, any material or immaterial object of experience. It is nothing more than this. Through our faculty of attention, we shift our minds from one object of experience to another object of experience; our attention continually changes from one object to another, and then to another. It is just the faculty of being attentive to what is happening. If we direct our attention towards remembering everything that happens, we shall remember everything that happens. Paying attention, *manasikāra*, is purely the turning of the mind towards an object of experience. We connect our minds with whatever object of experience we direct our attention towards. These objects of experience can be wholesome, unwholesome, or neutral. *Manasikāra* is not necessarily connected to a wholesome state of mind. This is not *sati*.

Sati is a wholesome state of mind, a wholesome conscious state of being, which is only ever associated with beneficial experience and is never associated with harmful experience. Entirely mindful of behaviour, people who maintain *sati* never let their minds fall away from a wholesome state. They are always directing their attention towards wholesome objects of experience. The guard at the entrance to their minds only opens the door to wholesomeness and never opens the door to unwholesomeness. If the man who forgets the bar of soap is a good meditator and is practising *sati* correctly, he is always turning his attention towards beneficial objects. He forgets the bar of soap simply because he does not turn his attention towards the bar of soap. Forgetting the bar of soap does not mean his mind is falling away from a wholesome state of being, from *sati*. It only means there was no attention paid to that particular object of experience, the bar of soap. Nothing more.

In translated western meditation books, I have read explanations of *sati* that cannot be agreed with whatsoever, not in the slightest. In one of these books, a conversation between a meditation student and his teacher is used to illustrate the concept of *sati*.

"Did you meditate?" asked the teacher.

"Yes," said the student. "I was practising *sati*."

"Where did you leave your shoes?"

"Near the door."

"Which side of the door?"

"I don't remember." The student forgets where his shoes are, but knows he took them off somewhere near the door.

"Then you have no *sati*," said the teacher. "Get out!" And the teacher chases the student away.

If the student were a good meditator, he did all of his actions with *sati* and it is still possible for him to have forgotten where he left his shoes. At the time he took off his shoes, he may have simply not directed his wholesome state of mind towards taking off his shoes. Nothing else. Because good meditators perform all of their activities—bathing, teeth brushing, removing shoes, or whatever—with a beneficial state of mind, they are performing their activities with complete *sati*. This student may have forgotten where he left his shoes simply because his *sati* was turned towards some other experience such as his mind and was not turned towards his shoes. Only that may have been lacking for this student. If this were the case, the student's mind did not fall away from wholesomeness. He did maintain his *sati*.

To teach these two separate concepts—*sati* and *manasikāra*—as if they were the same concept is a major mistake. *Sati* is different from *manasikāra*: a wholesome state of mind is not the same as simply paying attention to something. It took me a long time before I understood the difference between these two concepts. When I was a young meditator, I made the effort to perform all of my actions with a beneficial state of mind: without expectations and without letting my mind fall into an harmful state. But sometimes I forgot where I left some belonging of mine.

"You," said my teacher, "have no *sati*."

"What then," I asked, "is *sati* and what is just remembering everything?" I noticed I could be quite attentive while I performed unwholesome and harmful actions, and I also noticed I generally later remembered even these unwholesome and harmful actions. So however much I meditated, I had some doubt that *sati* was just being attentive and remembering, and this doubt became a problem for me. I respected my teachers because I knew they were teaching me in the correct way, but I had a problem with this particular aspect of their teachings that emphasised attention and remembering.

Only when I started to read the Tipiṭaka did I begin to understand the difference between *manasikāra* and *sati*. The Buddha spoke about *manasikāra* and *sati* as two separate topics. *Manasikāra* is quite different from *sati*. *Manasikāra* simply supports all of our states and actions. The guard's duty, our faculty of attention, is just to open and close the mind-door to the factors of the mind. That is all. Just be there and perform that duty: open and close the mind-door. *Manasikāra* helps us perform all of our actions, whether they are beneficial, neutral, or harmful. When *manasikāra* helps us to perform harmful actions, it is connecting with ignorance. *Sati*, on the other hand, never connects with ignorance and only supports the performance of wholesome actions. *Sati* only ever connects with wisdom, *paññā*. Nothing connects with *sati* except wisdom—absolutely nothing. This is what sets *sati* apart from *manasikāra*.

Admittedly, when we diligently train in paying attention to the objects of our experience, we develop a heightened level of mindful awareness that functions much like *sati*. Many years ago I trained in this *manasikāra* aspect of the teachings and now, if I decide from this moment on that I am going to pay good attention to every action I perform, every action I perform will be with an attentive state of mind. All of my physical actions—even the blinking of my eyes—will be experienced with good attention and afterwards I shall be able to recall most of these actions. But this is not *sati* as there is no development of wisdom, no progress.

Development requires turning our attention away from unwholesome objects and towards wholesome ones. When we do this, our attention is called *yoniso-manasikāra*. And because *sati* is always part of the state of mind associated with wholesomeness, *yoniso-manasikāra* supports the development of *sati*. Paying attention comes easily and automatically, but paying attention in a completely wholesome way, with *yoniso-manasikāra*, does not come automatically; it takes effort and development.

The Buddha once taught five hundred thieves. Having already developed their faculties of attention to very high levels, the thieves just needed the wisdom to turn their harmful attention into beneficial attention. Upon hearing the word of the Buddha, the thieves let go of their expectations and cravings, and they attained.

Clear Comprehension

When the Buddha described *sati*, he generally included the term *sampajañña*. *Sampajañña* means clearly seeing the characteristics of existence. With *sampajañña*, we are conscious of an experience as it arises and we are conscious of it as it passes away. *Sampajañña* is clear comprehension. There is a clarity of consciousness.

Connecting *sati* with *sampajañña*, *sati-sampajañña* means our wholesome state of mind and our clarity of consciousness are well developed; we never make a mind-state arise that is divorced from wholesomeness. We are fully aware of our actions and consider our actions, right in the midst of performing them, with wisdom. At this well-developed level of clarity, all of our physical actions, feelings, and mental states are wholesome. Every act and experience that takes place in our mental processes is made into something wholesome and beneficial. When we work with *sati-sampajañña*, we work with right understanding and right thought. We differentiate mentality from materiality, and we work with wisdom.

Each morning, the sun chases away the darkness of the night. We see objects that we didn't see during the night and there is no doubt in our minds as to the identity of these objects. There is no confusion. When the rays of the morning sun strike a pure dewdrop, the pure dewdrop gives a wonderful reflection of the morning sun. The light of the sun shines in the pure dewdrop.

The sun is *nibbāna*, darkness is ignorance, the pure dewdrop is a mind in *sati*, and seeing clearly is *sampajañña*. Purity combined with seeing clearly is *sati-sampajañña*. The pure, clear mind of *sati-sampajañña* is in the light of *nibbāna*. It is a bright state of mind. And, even though this state of mind is only a reflection of *nibbāna* and has not yet truly attained *nibbāna*, it shines just like *nibbāna* as it is not mixed up with any ignorance. A state full of wisdom, there is no confusion regarding experiences. Any object, anything, that comes into our field of experience is known without confusion. When we are in the light of *nibbāna*, in *sati-sampajañña*, we know the true nature of existence. The darkness of our ignorance is chased away and we see objects with clarity and understanding.

Another dewdrop is muddy. Not reflecting the morning sun, it is a mind mixed up with ignorance. With no *sati-sampajañña*, no wholesome state of mind and no clarity of consciousness, the muddy dewdrop never shines like *nibbāna*. Never.

When we train in *sati-sampajañña*, we act skilfully at all times in our lives, and easily make our way. We consider our meditation practice and our routine daily lives as one and the same, united. With our meditation practice woven into every part of our lives, we can be involved in any activity without conflict because we are always seeing clearly and are always free from expectations. When we have *sati-sampajañña*, we are the pure dewdrop and *nibbāna* shines.

Two kinds of people have *sati-sampajañña*: *arahats* and meditators who mindfully perform all of their actions without expectations. There is no clinging or aversion, only seeing clearly. To be free of suffering, we must develop our *sati-sampajañña*.

Four Foundations of Mindfulness

In the *satipaṭṭhāna-vipassanā* teachings of the Satipaṭṭhāna Sutta, the Buddha explains how we develop *sati-sampajañña*. He explains how we turn our bodies, our feelings, our states of mind, and the objects of our minds towards the wholesome and beneficial. The Buddha explains how we turn towards *sammā-sati* in order to overcome decay and death. The meditation practice taught by the Buddha in the Satipaṭṭhāna Sutta is a large comprehensive subject that is compared to an elephant's footprint: all other animals' footprints fit within an elephant's footprint. The *satipaṭṭhāna* practice is also compared to a large bowl into which all the other practices fit. We will not attempt an extensive discussion of the Satipaṭṭhāna Sutta; our discussion is limited to the practice of *sati* within the Satipaṭṭhāna Sutta.

Sati and *paṭṭhāna* are the two Pali words that combine to form *satipaṭṭhāna*. We know *sati* means a fully aware wholesome state of mind. *Paṭṭhāna* means establishment, attendance, waiting on. Thus literally, *satipaṭṭhāna* means establishing attention to a fully aware wholesome state of mind; although, *satipaṭṭhāna* is usually rendered as "foundations of mindfulness."

There are four foundations of mindfulness listed in the Satipaṭṭhāna Sutta:

1. Mindful contemplation of the body, *kāyānupassanā*
2. Mindful contemplation of feeling, *vedanānupassanā*
3. Mindful contemplation of states of mind, *cittānupassanā*
4. Mindful contemplation of mind-objects, *dhammānupassanā*

To develop our *sati*, we must develop beneficial attention, *yoniso-manasikāra*, towards the four foundations of mindfulness—body, feelings, states of mind, and mind-objects. Beneficial attention to the four foundations prevents us from misdirecting our attention towards the harmful.

Mindful Contemplation of the Body

The first foundation of mindfulness listed in the Satipaṭṭhāna Sutta is *kāyānupassanā*. *Kāya* means body and *anupassanā* means looking at, viewing, and contemplating with constant mindfulness. Putting the two terms together, *kāyānupassanā* is application of mindfulness to the contemplation of the body.

We use mindful contemplation of our bodies to turn all of our physical actions towards wholesomeness, and thus towards *sati*. This is accomplished through a number of exercises:

- Mindfulness of breathing, *ānāpānasati*
- Mindfulness of body postures, *iriyāpatha*
- Mindfulness with clear comprehension, *sati-sampajañña*
- Reflection on the thirty-two parts of the body, *kāyagatāsati* and *asubha*
- Analysis of the four physical elements, *dhātu-manasikāra*
- The nine charnel ground contemplations, *sīvathikā*

Mindful contemplation of the body, *kāyānupassanā*, means knowing the actions of our bodies as well as knowing the physical realities of our bodies; we dwell in mindful contemplation of the body, in the present. Truth has no past. Truth has no future. It will only be found in the present moment. We know what we are doing while we are doing it. When we drink a cup of tea, we are fully aware we are drinking a cup of tea; when we pick up a pen, we know we are picking up a pen; when we move the pen, we know we are moving it; and when we place the pen down, we also know we are placing it down. We are aware of our thoughts and intentions to pick the pen up, move it, and place it down. We get to the present. The past is gone. Through a variety of exercises, we get to the present.

Application of mindfulness to our breathing, *ānāpānasati*, is one of the exercises. We are aware of our breath as it goes in and aware of our breath as it goes out. We are aware of the rising and falling nature of our breathing.

Another exercise is the application of mindfulness to body postures, *iriyāpatha*. When we walk, we know we are walking; when we stand, we know we are standing; when we sit, we are aware and understand we are sitting; and when we lie down, we know we are lying down.

A third exercise is mindfulness with clear comprehension, *sati-sampajañña*. By being mindful of a bodily action at the same time we are engaged in that bodily action, we train in clear comprehension. When we go forward, we are aware we are going forward; when we go backward, we are aware we are going backward; and when we bend and stretch our limbs, we are aware we are bending and stretching our limbs. When we look straight ahead, we are aware we are looking straight ahead; when we look this way and that way, we are aware that we are looking this way and that way; when we turn our heads, we are fully aware we are turning our heads. Even when we blink, we do it with mindful awareness. We also eat and drink with awareness. We are aware of chewing our food, feeling the taste of our food, and swallowing our food. We are even aware of cleansing our bodies, going to the toilet, and taking care of personal needs.

By diligently training in clear comprehension, we develop the ability to habitually perform all of our bodily actions with a high level of awareness, with clear comprehension, with *sampajañña*. Clear comprehension of our actions enables us to convert all of our actions to wholesome and beneficial actions, and to live completely in the wholesome, in *sati*.

A fourth exercise is analysis of the four physical elements, *dhātu-manasikāra*: (1) earth, (2) water, (3) fire, and (4) air. With clear comprehension and understanding, we contemplate and come to know that our body is composed of the four physical elements; we know our body is the arising and the passing away of these four. With *sampajañña*, we are aware. There are just these primary elements in our bodies and the mind that is aware of them.

We are, for example, aware of the earth element in our bodies, a feeling of hardness. We just know that. We are simply aware that there is this feeling of hardness in our bodies. We do not feel adverse to that particular experience. No. We are just aware of the earth element and aware that the earth element has a feeling of hardness to it. We know that. Or we are aware of the water element in our bodies, a feeling of fluidity. We know we are sweating or that saliva is flowing in our mouths, and we know this is the water element. We are also aware of the fire element in our bodies, a feeling of heat. Heat is felt. There is the element of fire in our bodies and there is the mind that knows the element of fire in our bodies. And air element. We know, are aware that our breath goes in, know our breath goes out, and know this feeling of motion is the air element. We are aware of our bodies.

You are writing words in your notebook. A thought comes to you to write and then you are writing. And now, you know you are writing—you are writing with awareness. Because you are unsure about something I said, you put a question mark in your notebook. Doing your writing with full awareness is mindful contemplation of body.

When we apply mindful contemplation of body exercises—mindfulness of breathing, mindfulness of posture, and analysis of physical elements—throughout most of the day, we establish mindfulness on the body; we live in a mode of awareness. Continuously, again and again we practise being aware of our physical reality. If a physical action takes place, it takes place knowingly, with awareness of its physical reality. And thus, we are able to turn our bodies towards skilfulness. We turn towards *sati*. This is mindful contemplation of body, the first foundation of mindfulness.

While you are practising mindful contemplation of the body, the thought arises that this is good or this is bad: you are pleased or displeased with what you observe regarding the body. This quality, where the mental factor called feeling predominates, belongs to the Satipaṭṭhāna Sutta's mindful contemplation of feeling, *vedanānupassanā*, and it does not belong to mindful contemplation of the body. At the same time as you are practising mindful contemplation of the body, you are experiencing feeling, and are aware of it. Where and when this happens is subtle. The first foundation of mindfulness turns into the second foundation of mindfulness; mindful contemplation of the body turns into mindful contemplation of feeling. Your contemplation of feeling is actually going along together with your contemplation of body. Knowing this directly and experientially, *pajānāti*, requires very keen *sati*.

As I speak with you, I am experiencing mindful contemplation of feeling because I am wondering if what I am saying is being translated well and if you understand what I am saying. At this very moment, I am experiencing a feeling connected to whether or not you understand what I am teaching. When I think the teaching is being translated well and you understand the teaching, I experience the feeling as something pleasing. Mindful contemplation of feeling is present, feeling exists, in our experience with objects.

Though the Buddha spoke about the practice of mindful contemplation of the body, it is impossible to say that we are ever practising one hundred percent mindful contemplation of the body. Of course, we start off our practice by doing mindful contemplation of the body—that starting point is there—but feeling is always part of our experience. Therefore, we are also practising mindful contemplation of feeling at the same time as we are practising mindful contemplation of the body. And when we realise our mind is arising in this way, we are practising mindful contemplation of the states of mind, *cittānupassanā*.

Mindful contemplation of body, feeling, states of mind, and mind-objects—all four foundations of mindfulness are inseparably linked. The mindful contemplation of the body practice, for example, starts with mindful contemplation of the body, but then proceeds with mindful contemplation of the three other foundations. At the time we are performing any action, we know the physical action is one part, know the feeling of pleasure or pain connected with the action is another, and know it is the mind that is aware of these two distinct parts. Mindful contemplation of states of mind is knowing that it is the mind that knows the experience; mindful contemplation of mind-objects, *dhammā-nupassanā*, is knowing the mental experience arises and as soon as it arises it passes away.

When *sati* is good, all physical aspects of our lives, from the blinking of our eyes to the stretching of our arms, are clearly seen through the four foundations of mindfulness. We are aware of intentions, movements, speaking, wiping our eyes, our hand writing, and what is going on in our minds. When our mindfulness is more developed, we are also aware of the linking between the four foundations. We are completely aware of everything that takes place in our experience.

Mindful Contemplation of Feeling

The second foundation of mindfulness of the Satipaṭṭhāna Sutta is *vedanānupassanā*. *Vedanā* means feeling. Connecting *vedanā* with *anupassanā* yields *vedanānupassanā*, contemplating feelings with constant awareness. *Vedanānupassanā* is the application of mindfulness to the contemplation of feeling; we constantly contemplate and attend to feelings that arise from body and mind. There are five types of feelings

1. Pleasant bodily feeling, *kāyika sukha-vedanā*
2. Painful bodily feeling, *kāyika dukkha-vedanā*
3. Pleasant mental feeling, *cetasika sukha-vedanā*
4. Painful mental feeling, *cetasika dukkha-vedanā*
5. Equanimity, *upekkhā*

Feeling is the common factor. The first two types of feelings, pleasant and painful bodily feelings, pertain to physical feelings of the body, the materiality—*rūpa*. The third and fourth types, pleasant and painful mental feelings, pertain to psychological feelings, the mentality—*nāma*. Pleasant mental feelings include joy and painful mental feelings include frustrations and anger. The fifth type of feeling is equanimity. It is neutral. Neither pleasant nor painful bodily or mental feelings, it is a well-balanced mind free of aversion and clinging.

Due to a motorcycle accident, your friend's shoulder hurts and she is worried about it. Yes, she has an unpleasant feeling in her shoulder, but through worrying she has compounded her physical pain with psychological pain. We all have painful feelings in our bodies and do what we can to alleviate them. If necessary, we see a doctor. Physical pain in our bodies, however, is one thing. When we take our physical pains into our minds, when we think about them and are frustrated, our physical pains develop into psychological pains and that is a problem, an unnecessary problem. When your friend talks about her son, she forgets all of her pains. Thoughts of her son give her joy.

Do you remember the story of Devadatta throwing a stone at the Buddha? The Buddha's foot was injured, blood flowed, and *bhikkhus* carried him to see Dr. Jīvaka at the palace. After treatment, the Buddha returned to the monastery. That evening, the doctor became concerned and wanted to visit the Buddha, but the palace locked its gates at night and the doctor had to wait until the following morning.

"Did your injury cause you any pain last night?" asked Dr. Jīvaka.

"Yes," said the Buddha. "There was some pain in my foot, but none in my mind."

The Buddha experienced physical pain from his injury, but by no means did he allow his physical pain to disturb him mentally; his physical pain remained outside. For the Buddha, there was physical, but not psychological pressure. The same is said of *arahats*. They experience painful bodily feelings, but not painful mental feelings.

What do you mean by pressure?

We experience pressure from our psychological and physical burdens. This pressure is sometimes pleasant and sometimes painful. You, for example, experience pain when your friend tells you about the pain in her shoulder. Clearly, you are also experiencing pains when someone states views that are different from yours. At both of these times, you are experiencing painful mental feelings though you may also be experiencing some painful bodily feelings.

Is this psychosomatic pain?

You may be experiencing some painful feelings in your body, but in these two situations you are primarily experiencing painful mental feelings.

We practise mindful contemplation of our feelings, *vedanānupassanā*, in the same way we practise mindful contemplation of our bodies: we start with one foundation of mindfulness and then develop the three other foundations. Mindful contemplation of the body, for instance, begins by attending to the physical aspects of our bodies—eating, drinking, walking, breathing, the four elements, etc.—and then proceeds with mindful contemplation of feelings, states of mind, and finally mind-objects.

Mindful contemplation of feeling begins by applying mindfulness to the feelings that arise. We perceive whether our bodily or mental feelings are pleasant, painful, or neutral. Pleasant and painful feelings point out our mind. We clearly identify our pleasant, painful, and neutral feelings. Then we proceed with the remaining three foundations of mindfulness.

Often when we sit for meditation, our knees give us some pain. Perceiving this pain is mindful contemplation of feeling. We know this is a painful feeling. We also know this painful feeling arises in our knees, which is a part of our bodies. Knowing the pain is in the body is mindful contemplation of the body. Knowing whether our state of mind is wholesome and beneficial or unwholesome and harmful is mindful contemplation of states of mind. Finally, knowing the pain in our knees arises and also knowing it passes away is mindful contemplation of mind-objects. We know that our knee pain changes; it increases and decreases.

I don't like the pain from sitting.

As feelings are your own experience, nobody can tell you much about them. But investigate your feelings without attachment and ask yourself: "What is pain?"

Mindful contemplation of feeling enables you to see your feelings as they really are. Thus, when painful bodily feelings arise, you don't compound your physical pain with psychological pain. In its place, a deeper understanding of your pain develops.

Do I change my pain to pleasure or to a neutral feeling?

Just because you experience painful physical feelings, you do not necessarily have to experience painful mental feelings. You have a physical pain, but you are not suffering mentally. You recognise your painful physical feeling, see the reality of that painful feeling, and in this way turn your pain towards skilfulness.

Do I leave aside my pain?

To explain these details, I have to go into the Satipaṭṭhāna Sutta. Our discussion is limited to *sati*, *sati* within the eightfold path.

Mindful Contemplation of States of Mind

The Satipaṭṭhāna Sutta's third foundation of mindfulness is *cittānupassanā. Citta* translates as mind, consciousness, and states of consciousness; hence, *cittānupassanā* means contemplating mind with constant awareness. *Cittānupassanā* is the application of our mindfulness to the contemplation of states of mind, to our consciousness. We know that it is mind that perceives and understands any object.

And again, mindful contemplation of states of mind is practised in the same way we practise mindful contemplation of body and mindful contemplation of feeling: we begin with the specific foundation of mindfulness and then develop the other three foundations. With the mindful contemplation of states of mind practice, we start by applying mindful contemplation to our states of mind and then proceed to apply mindful contemplation to body, feelings, and mind-objects.

You seem to be thinking about your tape recorder. It is your mind that has the tape recorder as its object. Knowing that your mind has the tape recorder as its object is mindful contemplation of your state of mind; knowing that the tape recorder is made of physical elements is mindful contemplation of body; knowing the way you experience the tape recorder, what its value is for you and whether it gives you a pleasant or painful feeling, is mindful contemplation of feeling; and lastly, knowing that this is the arising of form and that this is the passing away of form is mindful contemplation of mind-objects. Change is happening. Mindful contemplation of mind-objects also includes knowing this is the arising of some concentration as well as knowing this is the passing away of concentration. Practising the four foundations in this way, we establish a fully aware wholesome state of mind.

Is contemplation of the tape recorder mindful contemplation of body, *kāyānupassanā*?

Yes. It falls in the analysis of the four physical elements, the *dhātu-manasikāra*, within mindful contemplation of body. At this point, the practice turns to mindful contemplation of mind-objects; *dhammānupassanā* grows here.

By constantly attending to and contemplating our states of consciousness, *cittānupassanā*, we are able to turn our minds away from unskilfulness, and turn our minds towards skilfulness. This is exactly the same as the body and the feelings practices: in the contemplation of body practice, we turn our bodies towards wholesomeness by performing physical actions without expectation; in the mindful contemplation of feelings practice, we turn our feelings to wholesomeness by seeing the reality of feeling. In the contemplation of states of mind practice, we turn our minds and thoughts to the wholesome and beneficial.

Mindful Contemplation of Mind-Objects

The fourth foundation of mindfulness listed in the Satipaṭṭhāna Sutta is *dhammānupassanā*. *Dhamma* as an object of mind can be anything past, present, or future, anything physical or mental, anything conditioned or unconditioned, and anything real or imagined. *Dhammānupassanā* is the contemplation of *dhamma*.

Dhammānupassanā is the application of mindfulness to the contemplation of various mind-objects:

- The five hindrances, *nīvaraṇa*
- The five aggregates, *khandha*
- The six internal and external sense bases, *saḷāyatana*
- The seven factors of enlightenment, *bojjhaṅga*
- The four noble truths, *ariya-sacca*

When *sati* is well developed, it is in the sphere of mindful contemplation of mind-objects where most contemplation takes place. Consider our minds to be water and our thoughts to be colouring. Pure water is colourless, odourless, and shapeless. When we add some dye to the water, the water takes on the colour of the dye. Nonetheless, there is still a difference between the water and the dye: water and dye are two separate and distinct entities. In the same way, when we engage in thinking, our minds take on the colour of our thoughts. Sometimes our thoughts support attaining *nibbāna* and sometimes our thoughts hinder attaining. Thoughts that are hindrances, *nīvaraṇa*, include excitement of sensual pleasures, ill will, dullness and lethargy, restlessness and worry, and doubt. Whether our thoughts support or hinder, there is still a difference between mind and thoughts. They are two separate entities.

Mindful contemplation of mind-objects, *dhammānupassanā*, means recognising whether hindrances are or aren't present in our minds. Is a hindrance to our attaining *nibbāna* on the rise? If so, how did it arise and how is it overcome? Mindful contemplation of mind-objects also includes recognising the characteristics of the five aggregates, the *khandhas*—feeling, perception, volitional formations, consciousness, and materiality. How do the aggregates arise and how do they pass away?

When our *sati* is good, we automatically turn our minds away from the hindrances. Automatically, we turn our minds towards the beneficial.

We hear a sound; a bird chirps. The object of our minds is the sound of the chirp, which is actually a form, a *rūpa*. At the very moment we hear the chirp, there is nothing else besides the sound of the chirp and the mind that knows the chirp. We feel the chirp is pleasant, painful, or neutral. We know the mind-object is feeling. We also know that our feeling towards the chirp arises and passes away, and we know that within our feelings there are various other thoughts taking place. All of this is mindful contemplation of mind-objects, *dhammānupassanā*.

Mindful contemplation of mind-objects means the object of the mind is mind. We are attentive and contemplate mind with mind as the mind changes from one object of experience to another object of experience to another.

Another example. With confidence in the teachings, we are working towards liberation, but for some reason anger arises. In the very moment that we are doing something with wisdom and understanding, we become overwhelmed, our confidence vanishes, and we get angry. In the next moment, our anger disappears and greed arises. The mind is changing from one object to another object. Our thoughts are changing.

Immediately recognising the thoughts that come to our mind, as soon as they come to mind, requires good mindfulness, *sati*. *Sati* enables us to know when anger is present in the mind and to know when greed is present. It enables us to immediately recognise whatever hindrance comes to our minds.

I often get very angry.

Sati enables you to see and note your harmful state of anger, and move on. This is similar to tasting sugar. A person can read about the taste of sugar, but it is quite different from actually tasting sugar. You are seeing your anger, not reading about it. Without *sati*, you never see your anger.

I am worried that my anger will explode and I will hurt someone.

Sati helps you to get through your anger because you are seeing your anger as it arises. Out of your craving, conceit, and views, you are clinging to something. You can see this for yourself. With *sati*, we recognise our hindrances in the same moment they arise and get rid of them, immediately. We use *sati* to let go of clinging and overcome our difficulties. It is almost useless to recognise hindrances after they have come and gone. No, that is not very useful. But for beginners, it is good enough.

Why is recognising my past hindrances any different from recognising my present hindrances?

When we reflect upon how our hindrances arose in the past, we improve our skill in recognising them when they arise in the present—we are developing our awareness, our *sati*. Eventually though, we need to recognise and dismantle our hindrances in the same moment they arise.

A flashlight helps us to find objects in the dark. When we shine the light, we see the object that we are looking for. Shining the light towards the object and seeing the object happen simultaneously in one and the very same moment. There aren't two moments. We shine the light into the dark place and at the exact same moment we see and recognise the object. Shining the light is mind and recognising the object is thought, all in one moment. Just as water is mind and coloured dye is thought, if we keep the mind clear, we are aware when any colour is added.

Keep the mind clear.

Yes. When we keep our minds clear and pure, we see when any colouring is added. Sometimes wholesomeness is added and sometimes unwholesomeness is added. Practising mindful contemplation of mind-objects means sorting out the mental factors that hinder our attaining of *nibbāna* from the mental factors that support our attaining, and then distancing ourselves from the factors that hinder. We purify our minds and turn our mental factors to the beneficial.

Essentially, this is what all four foundations of the Satipaṭṭhāna Sutta—mindful contemplation of body, feeling, states of mind, and mind-objects—accomplish. When we have *sati*, we are always in one of these four foundations. Sometimes we are in mindful contemplation of states of mind, sometimes feeling, sometimes body, and sometimes mind-objects. The meditator who meditates regularly and properly is always in one of the four foundations of mindfulness, lives in a wholesome state of mind, and is untouched by any unwholesomeness. The meditator is always in *sati*.

"All wholesome states of mind," said the Buddha, "are *sati*."

Again, how do we turn our lives towards the beneficial?

By performing actions, by experiencing feelings, and by experiencing mind-states without any expectations whatsoever, we turn towards the wholesome. We also turn towards the wholesome through confidence in whatever liberation it was that the Buddha found. We are confident the Buddha followed a certain path to make a particular state arise, and we are confident that state arose when he followed that path. This path is the eightfold path. This path is the four foundations of mindfulness. We are confident the Buddha followed this path and achieved liberation from suffering.

The Direct Path

The eightfold path is called the *ekāyana-magga*—the direct path. Nothing else gets mixed up with it. It is the straightest way to the goal. The way of the Buddha and the four foundations of mindfulness—these are the practices of a person on the direct path.

The person on the path lives alone. This does not mean retiring to the forest, isolation in a room, or anything like that. No. To the person living alone, the city is the same as the forest. *Eko vūpakaṭṭha appamatto ātāpi* is a frequently used expression to describe life on the path. And though *eko vūpakaṭṭha appamatto ātāpi* does include living alone, it also includes being zealous and being master of oneself. We are zealous in mastering the solitary life, a life of seclusion. This does not mean physically removing ourselves from other people. It does not mean that. Living alone means making the effort to restrain and abandon the harmful, as well as making the effort to develop and maintain the beneficial. Alone means unwholesomeness never accompanies us. Alone on the path, we neither judge nor criticise others.

"This path," said the Buddha, "is the only way to overcome *dukkha*."

A meditation centre is where people on the direct path live together. We practise living without expectations. When we eat our meals, we do not think about tomorrow's meal. Striving to maintain our minds and perform all of our actions in the present moment, the present moment is now. The next moment is also now. In this very moment, we try hard to prevent harmful states from arising. We do not allow greed to get mixed up with the present moment, do not allow aversion to get mixed up with the present moment, and do not allow delusion to get mixed up with the present moment. This is a practice of causes and effects, *hetu-phala*. Recognising and believing in causes and their effects is non-delusion, *amoha*.

Through contemplation and training, the *satipaṭṭhāna* practice develops. When we train properly for a month or two, without any gaps in the practice, our *sati* begins to function automatically. When we are firmly established in the four foundations of mindfulness, we know the state of *sati*.

What role do *jhānas* play in the foundations of mindfulness?

When we think of something, we are creating a body, a *kāya*, in our minds. This is a mental body, a mind created form. When we practise the *jhānas*, the sign of the *jhāna*—the *nimitta*—appears in our minds. This is also a mental body. A well-trained *jhāna-nimitta* can be used to practise psychic powers. For instance, if you were trying to find a particular person, you want the image of that person to appear within the *nimitta*. A type of light is created, which is then used to find the person. As part of the *satipaṭṭhāna-vipassanā* practice, these external bodies are noted as *dhammānupassanā*.

What about dreams?

A good meditator rarely dreams. But if a good meditator does dream, they note these mind created images as part of their *satipaṭṭhāna* practice; they note them in the same way they note any other phenomena. There is no difference between our waking state and our dream state. Our existence in this world is a dream. Mental bodies do not physically exist. They are mind created forms that we apprehend with our minds.

Many mind created forms, such as a *jhāna-nimitta*, are more difficult to let go of than the physical forms we usually encounter in this world because they arise when the hindrances are suppressed. There is a tranquillity, a satisfaction in the mind, and the meditator is not interested in directing his or her mind towards *nibbāna*.

"Regarding attainment of the earth kasiṇa as the supreme goal, some contemplatives generate this attainment. Others take one of the other kasiṇas as supreme—the water kasiṇa, the fire kasiṇa, etc.—and reach the corresponding meditative state. But for each kasiṇa, the Buddha has directly understood to what extent it is supreme, and having understood this, he saw its origin, he saw the danger, he saw the escape, and he saw the knowledge and vision of the true path and the wrong path. Having seen all this, he understood the attainment of the goal and the peace of the heart."

Venerable Mahā Kaccāna—Kali Sutta[22]

18 Right Concentration

Pemasiri Thera: The eighth factor of the noble eightfold path is right concentration, *sammā-samādhi*. It is more than just concentration.

Sammā-samādhi requires understanding and wisdom. It requires gradual training in observing rules of discipline, restraining our sense faculties, and abandoning our hindrances. For *sammā-samādhi* to arise, we need to be mindful and fully aware. We practise the four foundations of mindfulness: we live contemplating the body, feelings, states of mind, and mind-objects. When we practise in this way and attain the *jhānas*, *samādhi* is called *sammā-samādhi.*

Our minds are like round cooking pots: if unsupported, they are unstable and easily upset. To support and balance a pot, we place three stones under it. There is no use in placing only two stones under a round pot. No. To give a pot the proper support, we need to place three stones under it. When a round pot is properly supported, a fire can be made and a meal cooked.

Similarly, to support and balance our minds, we establish the first seven factors of the eightfold path—right understanding, right thought, right speech, right action, right livelihood, right effort, and right mindfulness. Each of the seven factors is important. When our minds are properly supported, they remain stable and right concentration arises. We are awake and see objects as they really are.

"*Sammā-samādhi*," said the Buddha, "is the collection of the first seven factors of the eightfold path."

Developing Concentration

For us to have a proper discussion on the development of concentration and the *jhānas*, we need to experience concentration and the *jhānas*. If the experiences from practice are lacking, it is impossible for the teacher to teach this subject and impossible for the student to truly understand it. We are not talking about the suttas. We are talking about training in specific practices. Since I am not practising the *jhānas* these days, I must try to recall the training that I went through when I was a young *bhikkhu* living in the forest. This is difficult.

That said, one-pointedness of mind, *citt'ekaggatā*, is our starting point for the development of concentration, *samādhi*. One-pointedness means there is unification between our minds and the object that stimulates our minds: we focus in on an object and at that exact moment only that one object is in our minds. A neutral factor of our mental processes, one-pointedness recognises and apprehends a range of objects. By repeatedly directing our minds towards a chosen object of perception, we increase the number of times we fully apprehend the chosen object. When we repeatedly apprehend the same object at a higher than ordinary rate, our one-pointedness develops into the state of *samādhi*. There is a significant increase in the number of times one-pointedness arises over a relatively brief interval of time.

When we look at the teacup on the table, our one-pointedness arises in connection with the teacup and we immediately recognise it. If we repeatedly direct our full attention towards the teacup, we increase the number of times our one-pointedness arises in connection with the teacup and decrease the number of times our one-pointedness arises in connection with other objects, and *samādhi* arises in connection with the teacup. If we are able to maintain *samādhi* for fifteen minutes with the teacup as our object, our one-pointedness might arise ten or fifteen times in connection with the teacup. The sign—teacup...teacup... teacup...teacup—is not continuously sustained in the mind for fifteen minutes.

DAVID: Why is the rate so low?

That rate is just an example. The number of times that one-pointedness arises in connection with the chosen object depends upon the individual meditator's practice. At the starting point of *samādhi*, a meditator's one-pointedness is weak. After practising with an object for a year, a meditator's one-pointedness could be very strong.

Beginning Concentration

Developing the strength of our concentration means developing the strength of the five *jhāna* factors:

1. Applied thought, *vitakka*
2. Sustained thought, *vicāra*
3. Rapture, *pīti*
4. Happiness, *sukha*
5. One-pointedness of mind, *citt'ekaggatā*

All five *jhāna* factors must be developed. With a wholesome state of mind, we apply our attention towards a suitable object of meditation. Next, we do some investigation and sustain our thoughts on the object. With the development of applied and sustained thought, rapture and happiness eventually arise. And because one-pointedness holds the mind on any object, it always accompanies the other four *jhāna* factors.

For example, if we were doing the practice of loving-kindness, we begin by applying and sustaining thoughts of loving-kindness towards ourselves.

I thought I directed thoughts of loving-kindness towards others.

Before we can feel loving-kindness for others, we must be able to feel loving-kindness for ourselves. How is it possible to make others happy when we are unhappy? We cannot give what we do not have.

When we have enough wisdom, we practise loving-kindness meditation, *mettā-bhāvanā*. Free from ill will, we fill our minds with thoughts of compassion and peace. We radiate thoughts of loving-kindness. We're concerned for the welfare of all beings. This is applied thought. It is just the initial directing of thoughts of loving-kindness towards all beings. By repeatedly directing thoughts of loving-kindness, we increase the number of times our one-pointedness of mind arises in connection with thoughts of loving-kindness and decrease the number of times our one-pointedness arises in connection with other thoughts; the *jhāna* factor of one-pointedness arises along with the *jhāna* factor of applied thought. Sustained thought furthers the process. There is an actual investigation of loving-kindness for beings. Sustained thought holds the one-pointed mind in directing loving-kindness towards the being. We stay within the subject of loving-kindness longer than we did with our initial thoughts of loving-kindness.

I am not following.

We are defining the *jhāna* factors. Striking a bell is applied thought and the ringing of the bell is sustained thought. We are striking at suitable objects of meditation with applied thought. A hawk flapping its wings is applied thought, and its soaring through the sky is sustained thought. And with *mettā-bhāvanā*, applied thought means directing the mind onto thoughts of loving-kindness towards the being; it is just the initial application. Sustained thought, on the other hand, means the mind is held in thoughts of loving-kindness towards the being. Sustained thought is a more developed and stable state than applied thought. By making the effort to apply and sustain thoughts of loving-kindness towards beings, the remaining two *jhāna* factors, rapture and happiness, are aroused. In the beginning level of concentration, all five *jhāna* factors arise but at low levels of strength. There is lightness in mind and body.

Directing our thoughts towards an object of meditation does not mean we never think of anything but the object of meditation. Various thoughts do arise in our minds, but the majority of them are connected with the main object; we don't let our minds wander too far. For example, while doing the practice of loving-kindness we may think of work, a trip we are about to take, or the clothes we hung out to dry. When distracting thoughts such as these arise, we let them go and return to directing our thoughts of loving-kindness towards all beings. When we direct and sustain thoughts of loving-kindness in this way, our mental factor of one-pointedness is, for most of the time, in loving-kindness. It's as if our mind's attention is limited to the area within a circle: our minds do not go outside that circle. But it is not that our minds are completely hidden away in only one place.

Neighbourhood Concentration

When the meditator maintains his or her mind for longer and longer periods of time on a suitable object of meditation, the five *jhāna* factors strengthen and the hindrances weaken. Sometimes the meditator's applied and sustained thought are strong, but rapture and happiness are not quite so strong; at another time it could be that rapture and happiness are strong, but applied and sustained thought are slightly weaker; possibly one-pointedness is the strong *jhāna* factor. This is neighbourhood *samādhi*, *upacāra-samādhi*. All five *jhāna* factors are arising at high levels of strength for the meditator, but they are arising at somewhat unbalanced levels.

Neighbourhood *samādhi* is the level of concentration that precedes entering *jhāna*. In neighbourhood *samādhi* the meditator comes to feel the presence of all five *jhāna* factors. He or she realises their mind keeps turning towards the chosen object, is with the object for extended periods, and is not scattered about in other objects. From time to time, they recognise the *jhāna* factors of applied and sustained thought, and they also recognise rapture and happiness. They are aware of lightness in body and mind. Achieving a rough idea of the quality of the *jhāna* state, they realise *jhāna* factors are actually arising in their mental processes. The arising of *jhāna* factors indicates the gaining of neighbourhood *samādhi* for the teacher and the meditator.

Meditators often know they are in neighbourhood *samādhi*, but seldom know exactly what they need to do to go beyond neighbourhood *samādhi* and attain *jhāna*. The meditator just knows that everything is a little bit off. This is like a person trying to enter this meditation hall. The person walks along the right road, enters through the main gate, and walks up to the base of the steps at the front of the hall. The person may even walk up the steps, but fails to take the last step into the meditation hall. The person is very close to the meditation hall and gains some idea of what the hall is like, but never completely enters into the hall. He or she only stands on the top step for a while, and then goes home.

Attainment Concentration

Before meditators attain *jhāna*, they must balance the *jhāna* factors of their neighbourhood *samādhi*. It is this way for everyone. Possibly training with one object of meditation for a whole year, the meditator tries to direct their *jhāna* factors in a strong and completely balanced way. During most of that year, a strong meditator would be in neighbourhood *samādhi*.

If loving-kindness is the meditator's object, he or she directs thoughts of loving-kindness towards beings, "May all beings be well and free from suffering." When thoughts of loving-kindness are sustained in the mind of the meditator for longer and longer periods of time, one-pointedness arises together with applied and sustained thoughts of loving-kindness. Further training leads to rapture and happiness arising, and stronger one-pointedness. When all five of their *jhāna* factors arise at one strong level, a moment of absorbed consciousness suddenly arises, and they reach attainment *samādhi*, *appanā-samādhi*.

Attaining *jhāna* for the first time is like walking along a city street and coming across a crack: we stop walking the way we usually do and jump over the crack. After the crack, we resume our usual way of walking. We might not even notice that we jumped the crack.

In our everyday lives, we continually relate to sense objects according to our cravings for sensual pleasures; our minds flow along the street of the sense-sphere realm of existence, the *kāmā-loka*. In neighbourhood *samādhi*, a meditator's cravings for sensual pleasures are suppressed by the *jhāna* factors, but the factors are arising at somewhat unbalanced levels of strength, which means he or she is also still in the sense-sphere realm of existence. When all five of their *jhāna* factors arise at one balanced and high level of strength, there is a complete suspension and interruption of ordinary sense activity. The meditator leaves the sense-sphere realm behind and enters into the fine-material realm, *rūpā-loka*. *Jhāna* is attained.

Attainment into the fine-material realm lasts for just a few mind-moments, not even one full second. After attainment, the meditator simply returns to neighbourhood *samādhi*: *jhāna* factors continue to arise, but at slightly unbalanced levels of strength. And because the *jhāna* lasted for such a brief period of time, the meditator is likely unaware they balanced the *jhāna* factors and attained *jhāna*.

After leaving the *jhāna*, are the *jhāna* factors strong?

The *jhāna* factors remain strong and stable, sometimes continuing to arise off and on for half a day. While eating, going to the toilet, and talking with someone—all five *jhāna* factors of neighbourhood *samādhi* continue to arise.

If the *jhāna* factors have not dispersed, another person's actions cannot cause any anger to arise. When you see a meditator getting angry and yelling at someone who is making noise, the meditator is holding onto only one of his or her five *jhāna* factors, such as one-pointedness. The meditator gets angry because the noise breaks his or her single *jhāna* factor. Earlier, I shouted at the person who slammed a door. If I have a *jhāna* practice and all five of my *jhāna* factors are aroused, my hindrances are suppressed and I do not get angry. If someone disturbs me now, I shout at them.

When a teacher sees the meditator's five *jhāna* factors are remaining strong and stable, the teacher knows the *jhāna* must have been attained. In contrast, the meditator rarely knows he or she has attained *jhāna* for the first time because the meditator experiences the *jhāna* for only a few mind-moments and then immediately returns to neighbourhood *samādhi*: the *jhāna* factors continue to arise at high, although at somewhat unbalanced, levels of strength. Many meditators think they are in *jhāna* when their *jhāna* factors are arising at very high levels, but the form of concentration existing during *jhāna* is radically different from the concentration of neighbourhood *samādhi.*

To develop the *jhāna*, meditators train to make *jhāna* mind-moments arise more regularly and to maintain them for longer periods. By fixing their attention on one of the objects of *samatha* meditation, meditators gradually increase their time of *samādhi*. Little by little, they gain more and more control over their chosen object. They learn how to make the object arise quickly in their minds and how to stabilize the object when it arises in their minds. They increase their time of suspension from the sense-sphere realm.

First Fine-Material *Jhāna*

The nature of the first *jhāna* is like eating an enjoyable meal. We are hungry. We direct our minds towards something we like to eat, such as a mango. This is applied thought. As we eat the mango, our minds are with the mango, not scattered about in other things. We only have thoughts of how good the mango tastes. This is sustained thought. And because we are applying and sustaining all of our thoughts towards the mango, a kind of rapture and happiness arises. Sinking into the experience of eating the mango, we almost forget that our minds and bodies exist.

Do sounds disturb the *jhāna*?

Sounds need not disturb the first *jhāna* because the mind is stable at that level of concentration, and this world of the five senses is forgotten. At this moment, for example, you can hear the workmen building a new room. They are talking, cutting boards, hammering nails, and making all sorts of sounds. While sitting in *jhāna*, we might hear these types of sounds but our *jhāna* factors are only directed towards the object of the *jhāna* and are not directed towards other objects, such as the sounds these workmen are making.

Many people have the impression the first *jhāna* state of consciousness is rock solid and that nothing else happens. This is a misconception. If while sitting in the first *jhāna* a large branch breaks off a tree and falls to the ground with a loud crash, we hear the sound of the crash and then immediately return to *jhāna*. When we get up from the sit, however, we have forgotten that we heard the sound of crash. But we did hear the crash. At the moment the branch hit the ground, we were aware of the sound of the crash but our mind wasn't further applied to that sound. If someone tells us that a branch crashed to the ground while we sat, we may remember that we heard it.

Even in city meditation centres, the first *jhāna* can be attained quite quickly. It is, however, impossible to maintain *jhāna* in most city centres because the external environment is unsuitable. Say, for example, you attain to a *jhāna* state of mind. This is just an example. A friend comes by and starts talking with you. When you talk with your friend, you lose control of the *jhāna*. You cannot make the *jhāna* arise at will and you cannot maintain the *jhāna*. But if you avoid talking with your friend, he gets angry. He assumes you are not talking with him because you are conceited; you have *māna*. These types of personal situations make it difficult to maintain the *jhāna* in city centres—they destroy the *jhāna* state of mind.

To maintain the mind in *jhāna,* we have to go to the forest. We do not go to the forest to just attain *jhāna.* No. After having attained *jhāna,* we go to the forest to develop, strengthen, and maintain it. In the forest, meditators train their minds to be calm and concentrated. They become familiar with their object of meditation, make the *nimitta* sign of the object arise when they choose to make it arise, and it arises quickly. They become skilled in attaining and remaining in *jhāna*. This is called mastery, *vasī.* When meditators succeed in realising a completely firm *jhāna* state of mind, it is called *jhāna-samāpatti*. Their minds are fully settled down in the state of *samādhi.* They realise all four *jhānas* and can use the *jhāna* for many purposes, such as developing psychic powers and strengthening their *vipassanā*.

Many meditators attain *jhāna* but roughly only one in 100,000 meditators will develop the state of *jhāna* up to the *samāpatti* level. Meditators who have only *samādhi*, and have not completely settled down their minds in the state of *samādhi* to the *samāpatti* level cannot make their meditation object arise quickly or at will. Although their unwholesome states will be suppressed, they cannot use the *jhāna* for any purpose.

Higher Fine-Material *Jhānas*

In the Mahāsatipaṭṭhāna Sutta of the Dīgha Nikāya, the Buddha states that *sammā-samādhi* is entering into and remaining in the four fine-material mental absorptions, the *rūpa-jjhānas*:

- First fine-material mental absorption, *paṭhamajjhāna*
- Second fine-material mental absorption, *dutiyajjhāna*
- Third fine-material mental absorption, *tatiyajjhāna*
- Fourth fine-material mental absorption, *catutthajjhāna*

In the first *jhāna,* all five *jhāna* factors are at work suppressing hindrances. Applied thought, sustained thought, rapture, happiness, and one-pointedness of mind—all five are strong, steady, and evenly balanced.

To progress to the higher *jhānas,* meditators refine each *jhāna* and eliminate its *jhāna* factors. Progression is nothing more than that. As the meditator enters the second *jhāna,* applied and sustained thought are eliminated; as the meditator enters the third, rapture is eliminated; and upon entering the fourth, happiness turns to equanimity. In the fourth *jhāna*, the meditator is left with only equanimity and one-pointedness of mind. See Table 1.

Table 1: The Four *Jhāna* System

		First	***Second***	***Third***	***Fourth***
Jhāna Factor	**Applied Thought**	Working	Eliminated	Eliminated	Eliminated
	Sustained Thought	Working	Eliminated	Eliminated	Eliminated
	Rapture	Working	Working	Eliminated	Eliminated
	Happiness	Working	Working	Working	Eliminated
	One-pointedness of mind	Working	Working	Working	Working

The Abhidhamma lists five instead of four *jhānas*. In its system, all five *jhāna* factors are again at work in the first *jhāna*, but later on applied thought drops off. See Table 2.

Table 2: The Five *Jhāna* System

Jhāna Factor		First	Second	Third	Fourth	Fifth
	Applied Thought	Working	Eliminated	Eliminated	Eliminated	Eliminated
	Sustained Thought	Working	Working	Eliminated	Eliminated	Eliminated
	Rapture	Working	Working	Working	Eliminated	Eliminated
	Happiness	Working	Working	Working	Working	Eliminated
	One-pointedness of mind	Working	Working	Working	Working	Working

Why does applied thought drop off?

Applied thought is unnecessary because after a while you know what you are doing. Until a bee finds a flower, it has to go searching here and there. Once the bee finds the flower, the bee goes directly to it. And when meditators become skilled in the first *jhāna*, they no longer need applied thought on the object. Their one-pointedness is strong enough to hold the object and they go directly into sustained thought on the object. Meditators who attain the first *jhāna* find a wholesome quality of mind that is comparable to the mind of an *anāgāmī*. When meditators stop their *jhāna* practice, however, they lose this wholesome quality; an *anāgāmī* doesn't.

To progress through the four *jhāna* system using loving-kindness meditation, the meditator reaches the loving-kindness of the first *jhāna* by directing applied and sustained thoughts of loving-kindness towards all beings. With continued practice, he or she masters entering and remaining in the experience of the first *jhāna*. It becomes a habit.

To progress from the first to the second *jhāna*, the meditator must eliminate the first *jhāna's* original two *jhāna* factors—applied and sustained thought. Because the meditator has successfully entered into the first *jhāna* over and over again, he or she can let applied and sustained thought drop off and reach the loving-kindness of the second *jhāna* through its *jhāna* factor of rapture.

When the second *jhāna* is mastered and refined, the meditator can let its nature of rapture drop off, and he or she reaches the loving-kindness of the third *jhāna* through happiness and one-pointedness.

Now, the only *jhāna* factors in the third *jhāna* are happiness and one-pointedness, a feeling of comfort in the mind of the meditator. And using loving-kindness as the object of meditation, the third *jhāna* is the highest state of consciousness that can be reached. Many meditators stop at the third *jhāna.*

To progress from the third to the fourth *jhāna,* meditators must abandon the *jhāna* factor of happiness. They have to let go of their sense of comfort and just be with equanimity. To do this, the meditator changes the object of his or her meditation from loving-kindness to equanimity. Happiness then drops out of the mind and in its place the equanimity of the fourth *jhāna* arises.

The fourth *jhāna* is a combination of equanimity and one-pointedness of mind. When meditators enter the fourth *jhāna*, they realise what is in the books is exactly the same as what they have experienced: progression through the *jhānas* is nothing more than refining and eliminating *jhāna* factors from the initial five down to one-pointedness, and equanimity.

The teachings of the Buddha found in the Mahāsatipaṭṭhāna Sutta are unnecessary for the development and attainment of *jhāna*. They are not essential. In many other religious traditions, *jhāna* states of consciousness are developed and attained.

Why do people want to attain the higher *jhānas*?

Meditators want to proceed to the higher *jhānas* because they prefer the *jhāna's* wholesome and refined state of consciousness to their worldly and ordinary state of consciousness. The consciousness found in the first *jhāna* is, however, dangerously close to the ordinary state. At any time in the first *jhāna*, novice meditators can lose their *jhāna* state of consciousness and fall back to their sense-sphere realm state of consciousness. They want to avoid this. Secondly, after emerging from the first *jhāna*, meditators see the *jhāna* factors clearly and realise the first *jhāna's* factors of applied and sustained thought are crude and disturbing when compared to its factors of rapture and happiness. Knowing applied and sustained thought are absent from the second *jhāna,* meditators set out to attain the second.

To rise from the first to the second *jhāna*, meditators let go of their attachment to the first *jhāna* and get into the neighbourhood *samādhi* of the second *jhāna*. All five *jhāna* factors of the ordinary sense-sphere realm way of thinking are again briefly present with the purpose in mind of abandoning the two crude *jhāna* factors and attaining the second *jhāna*. Onwards into the second *jhāna*, the meditator's ordinary sense-sphere realm way of thinking is interrupted and he or she enters into the second *jhāna* of the fine-material realm. After the interruption, the three *jhāna* factors of the second are clearly seen.

To rise from the second to the third *jhāna*, meditators let go of the second *jhāna*, work the neighbourhood *samādhi* of the third *jhāna*, and then enter the third. Proceed. Go on like that. Give up the third *jhāna*, again the neighbourhood *samādhi*, and then enter the fourth *jhāna*.

Attainment of each level of *jhāna* is dependent upon understanding and mastering each immediately preceding level of *jhāna*; the *jhānas* develop in stages. After emerging from each *jhāna*, meditators reflect back on its unique dangers and drawbacks. Upon reflecting back on the first *jhāna*, for example, meditators see that it is dangerously close to the hindrances of the sense-sphere realm and has the drawback of applied and sustained thought. Meditators want to overcome coarse states of consciousness and attain more peaceful and refined states. Despite having these goals, meditators are not actually trying to gain something. No. They keep their object of meditation and refine their *jhāna* factors. If there is attachment and high expectations, meditators cannot progress. Meditators must always reflect back and clearly see the disgusting aspect of these refined states of consciousness.

In Sri Lanka, many meditators have powerful *samādhi* and have attained to the fourth *jhāna*. Because that state of consciousness is very refined, they often think they are *arahats* and stop meditating altogether. But they are not necessarily *arahats*.

Are they *sotāpannas*?

When meditators are in the fourth *jhāna*, their hindrances are suppressed. Nothing more. This is different from attaining path and fruit, *magga-phala*.

At the time of the Buddha, two groups of 500 *bhikkhus* were on a trip together. Through meditation on the divine abodes, the first group had attained to the fourth *jhāna;* the second group had somehow attained to *arahatship*. When the combined group of 1000 *bhikkhus* met some *devas*, the *devas* only paid respects to the first group who had attained to the fourth *jhāna*, and they ignored the *arahats*. The *devas* paid respects to the first group because they felt the loving-kindness radiating from these *bhikkhus*. But being only *devas,* they were unable to feel completely liberated minds.

Another story: a *bhikkhu* thought he was an *arahat* because he had the fourth *jhāna.* A good friend of his who actually was a *sotāpanna* often tried to explain that just having the fourth *jhāna* did not mean he was an *arahat*. But the *bhikkhu* did not believe his friend. One day, the two men were bathing in a river. Without the *bhikkhu* who had the fourth *jhāna* noticing, his friend the *sotāpanna* dove below the surface of the water and bit the *bhikkhu's* leg. The *bhikkhu* screamed. Thinking a crocodile was attacking, he rushed out of the river and ran up the bank.

"See," said the *sotāpanna*, "you are afraid. If you were an *arahat,* you would be fearless and would never scream." Because of the experience, the *bhikkhu* realised he was not an *arahat.* He returned to his practice and finally attained *arahatship.*

When the fourth *jhāna* is well balanced and firm, it is called fourth *jhāna samāpatti.* Just as water in a stream flows down various channels, the fourth *jhāna* is an especially pure state of consciousness from which the meditator directs his or her practice down one of three channels: produce psychic powers, attain the immaterial *jhānas*, or go straight towards *nibbāna* with *vipassanā.*

Choosing to produce psychic powers, meditators hear subtle sounds and see things that are normally invisible. They have the power to see past lives and travel in space. The fourth *jhāna samāpatti* is a junction.

Where you can make a choice?

Yes.

What role do the four foundations of mindfulness play?

When you practise the *satipaṭṭhāna* properly, you get into the fourth *jhāna samāpatti.* And though it is difficult to *maintain* the fourth *jhāna*, it is not extremely difficult to simply *attain* it. Attaining is easier than maintaining. Living in a forest helps.

Immaterial *Jhānas*

Upon emerging from the fourth fine-material *jhāna*, meditators reflect back and realise the fourth *jhāna* has its drawbacks: it is still dependent upon materiality and is close to the third *jhāna's* relatively crude *jhāna* factor of happiness. Knowing materiality to be absent from the immaterial *jhānas,* meditators set out to attain the more refined and peaceful states of the four immaterial *jhānas, arūpa-jjhānas*:

- First immaterial *jhāna*: the sphere of boundless space, *ākāsānañcāyatana*
- Second immaterial *jhāna*: the sphere of boundless consciousness, *viññāṇañcāyatana*
- Third immaterial *jhāna*: the sphere of nothingness, *ākiñcaññāyatana*
- Fourth immaterial *jhāna*: the sphere of neither-perception-nor-non-perception, *nevasaññā-n'āsaññāyatana*

The immaterial *jhānas* are different from the fine-material *jhānas*. In the four fine-material *jhānas*, meditators keep their object of meditation and progress through the fine-material *jhānas* by overcoming the *jhāna* factors. They keep the same object. In the immaterial *jhānas*, on the other hand, meditators progress through the four immaterial *jhānas* by overcoming each preceding *jhāna's* object.

Progression through the immaterial *jhānas* happens gradually. By shifting attention away from the relatively coarse object of the preceding *jhāna* and directing it towards the more refined object of the next *jhāna*, the coarse object gradually fades. The meditator continues to concentrate solely on the refined object until the coarse object is completely overcome, and only the refined object remains.

Before meditators can attempt the immaterial *jhānas,* however, they must have mastery of the fourth fine-material *jhāna*, which means not only attainment of the fourth but also control. They must be able to enter it at will and be able to stay in its experience. In the fourth fine-material *jhāna*, the meditators' *jhāna* factors of one-pointedness and equanimity are established, their in-and-out breathing ceases, and their minds do not go out towards external objects. In the fourth, meditators contemplate the nature of form and reality. There is just consciousness and nothing to consider about the physical body.

With a *kasiṇa nimitta* as the cause, the immaterial *jhānas* arise as the fruit. The *kasiṇa* might be a blue disc. The *nimitta* is a totality sign, such as a light, that arises in the meditator's mind. For instance, through observing the blue *kasiṇa*, the meditator makes the *kasiṇa's nimitta* arise and then expands it. The *nimitta* is expanded without limit, boundless. The meditator then progresses through the fine-material *jhānas* to the fourth.

To rise from the fourth fine-material *jhāna* to the first immaterial *jhāna*, the meditator needs to overcome his or her *nimitta*.

Concentrating only on the space that the *nimitta* occupies, the meditator thinks: "Boundless space. Space. Space is boundless." Gradually, the *nimitta* fades from the meditator's mind. Not all at once. After a long period of concentration on space, the meditator feels he or she is being blown away by a strong wind. The meditator continues to concentrate on space until all perceptions of gross and fine material forms, including the mind-created form of the *nimitta,* are blown away.

Now, because there are no forms in the meditator's mind, consciousness takes boundless space as its object of experience. Neither a sky type of space with clouds, nor a cosmic type of space with stars and planets, the space of the first immaterial *jhāna* is free of such things. Look at the air just in front of you. Your consciousness has that space as its object. It is fixed on space and nothing else. Nothing else. There are no thoughts about the physical body. No.

The meditator experiences space as something enormous. No end to it. You cannot think that space has a limit. To whatever extent is consciousness, to that extent is space. The consciousness of your mind is just in this vast empty space. There is only consciousness and space. And life. Life, consciousness, and space.

To overcome boundless space, meditators reflect that boundless space isn't as peaceful as boundless consciousness. Knowing boundless space has this drawback, they concentrate on the consciousness that had space as its object. They shift their attention to consciousness. Meditators think, "Consciousness. Consciousness."

By concentrating solely on the consciousness, the perception of being in boundless space gradually, very gradually, fades out of the meditator's mind until only consciousness remains.

You've lost me.

In the first immaterial *jhāna*, the meditator has boundless space as the object of his or her meditation. Boundless space is the experience, the object of consciousness. Without obstruction, boundless space extends as far as the meditator can extend his or her consciousness, which means the consciousness that apprehends boundless space as its object must also be boundless.

To reach the second immaterial *jhāna*, meditators take that particular boundless consciousness as the object of their meditation. They direct their attention to the consciousness that had boundless space as its object. Thus, boundless consciousness is the object of consciousness. Consciousness is the object of consciousness.

The meditator continues to concentrate on that boundless consciousness until boundless space is overcome, fades out completely. The meditator is then left with only the boundless consciousness—the second immaterial *jhāna* is reached.

The second immaterial *jhāna,* also called the sphere of boundless consciousness, has a more refined and peaceful nature than the sphere of boundless space.

To reach the third immaterial *jhāna*, the meditator reflects on the nature of consciousness. When consciousness is absent, there is nothing whatsoever. The meditator then takes the absence of consciousness to be his or her object of meditation. The meditator thinks, "There is nothing. Nothing whatsoever."

Concentrating solely on nothingness, consciousness then gradually fades away until there is nothing. The mind perceives there is nothing whatsoever, not even consciousness. The only perception in the mind is that there is nothing.

Remaining in the experience, the meditator finds nothingness to be a more refined and peaceful object for the mind than either boundless space or boundless consciousness. The meditator also finds that the emptiness of nothingness is different from the emptiness—the unobstructed vastness—of boundless space. He or she has no applied thoughts or even anything to think about.

With the fading away and overcoming of nothingness, the meditator reaches a deeply peaceful state. Not a state of enjoyment, it is more a state of appreciation. The meditator finds this to be the highest state possible and that nothingness was coarse in comparison. It is a state that has nothing to do with materiality. There is life, a vitality.

After attaining the fourth immaterial *jhāna*, meditators train upwards and downwards in all four immaterial *jhānas*. And then they train in attaining all eight *jhānas*—the four fine-material and four immaterial—in forward order and in reverse order. Up and down. To perform psychic powers, meditators work from the fourth *jhāna* of the fine-material level. They do not perform them from the immaterial level.

In the Aṅguttara Nikāya, the Buddha says the *jhānas* are a form of *nibbāna* that meditators can experience here and now. They use them to enjoy a pleasant abiding.

Do many meditators attain the *jhānas*?

Yes. Even before the Buddha began teaching, many people had searched for and found the *jhānas*. Given that at this time we have access to the Buddha's teachings, the *jhānas* are even easier to attain than before. If you think the *jhānas* are difficult to attain, you are mistaken.

How can this be?

The most difficult part of the practice is the initial suppression of the hindrances. After the hindrances are suppressed, there is no real problem and progression through the *jhānas* will just happen. Cutting down trees, blasting rocks, and filling mud-holes—building a road through dense jungle is difficult work. After the road is built, however, anyone can easily travel through the jungle. And after the hindrances are suppressed, the first *jhāna* can be attained. The rest of the *jhānas* aren't so difficult to attain either.

Why are the higher *jhānas* easy to attain?

Because meditators have already done the work required to suppress their hindrances, attaining the higher fine-material and then the immaterial *jhānas* is fairly straightforward. At the beginning of the practice, all meditators must exert a lot of effort to suppress their hindrances.

Attaining a *jhāna* state of consciousness is quite different from maintaining the mind in a *jhāna* state. The mere attainment of *jhāna* is not actually so difficult. But because *jhāna* states of consciousness are fragile, it is difficult to maintain them. These refined states collapse very easily.

What do you mean by collapse?

The meditator drops out of the fine-material realm of the *jhāna* and returns to his or her ordinary and everyday life. Back in the sense-sphere realm, the meditator's sense activity is again coarse and often unsatisfactory. The *dukkha* is there. When meditators can attain but not maintain the *jhāna,* they often become discouraged. Many conclude that meditating is pointless and completely give up their practice.

That's too bad.

Despite the *jhānas'* extreme degree of mental refinement, they are still nothing more than states of consciousness. Their attainment is not the goal of the practice.

Do you remember the man who came across a pile of rotting garbage?

Yes. He dug into the pile and cleared his path.

When meditators use only *samatha-bhāvanā* to gain *samādhi*, they are just covering up their garbage. To dig out their garbage and gain *sammā-samādhi*, meditators practise *vipassanā-bhāvanā* in combination with *samatha-bhāvanā.* This is the method of meditation taught by the Buddha in the Satipaṭṭhāna Sutta.

To suppress their hindrances, the meditator initially uses only *samatha* meditation; their method is completely *samatha* at the beginning. After their hindrances are suppressed, however, the meditator alternates *vipassanā* with *samatha* to attain and master all four fine-material *jhānas*. Letting go of the *jhānas,* the meditator then proceeds from the fourth fine-material *jhāna* without using it to produce psychic powers or to attain the immaterial *jhānas.*

Why doesn't the meditator attain the immaterial *jhānas*?

The *sammā-samādhi* of the Satipaṭṭhāna Sutta is only up to the fourth fine-material *jhāna samāpatti.* Not beyond that. Proceeding from the fourth fine-material *jhāna,* the meditator continues to strengthen his or her *samatha* and to further develop his or her *vipassanā*. Through personal experience, the meditator gains insight into how things really are—impermanent, unsatisfactory, and insubstantial. By penetrating the true nature of all conditioned phenomena, the meditator develops wisdom, overcomes the attachment to self, and moves closer to *nibbāna.* Once confidence is developed, it is easy to see what is correct and what is incorrect.

We have now finished the four noble truths and the noble eightfold path. Is there anything else you want to ask?

I don't know what to ask. I'm still working on *sīla*.

That's fine. When people have a sincere interest in *dhamma,* I enjoy teaching.

Thank you. I haven't entered the *jhānas*, not yet.

But you like to learn.

Glossary

Notes

An English-Pali and Pali-English Glossary

This glossary consists of the English terms and phrases that were used in this work as translations to replace Pali terms. It is an English-Pali and Pali-English glossary. The translations came primarily from three dictionaries: (1) Pali Text Society's *Pali-English Dictionary*, (2) Venerable Nyanatiloka's *Buddhist Dictionary: Manual of Buddhist Terms and Doctrines*, and (3) Bhikkhu Ñāṇamoli's *A Pali-English Glossary of Buddhist Technical Terms*.

A

Action: *Kamma*

Activities that lead to birth among animals: *Tiracchāna-gāminī paṭipadā*

Aggregates, five groups of existence or clinging: *Upādānakkhandha*—materiality, feeling, perception, volitional formations, and consciousness

Akusala: Unwholesome, unskilful, harmful

Almsgiving: *Dāna*

Anāgāmi: One realises the state of non-returner and is fully free from the first five lower fetters

Anatta: Non-self, insubstantiality

Anicca: Impermanence

Animal world: *Tiracchāna yoni*

Annihilationist view: *Uccheda-diṭṭhi*

Apāya: The lower worlds

Applied thought: *Vitakka*

Arahant: Synonymous with *arahat*

Arahat: One who realises the state of holiness and is free from all ten fetters

Ārammaṇa: Object

Ariya: Noble

Arūpa-loka: Immaterial realm

Arūpa-rāga: Immaterial realm passion

Asubha: *Subha* is usually defined as the pleasure taken from objects. *Asubha* is seeing the reality of pleasurable objects.

Attainment of cessation: *Nirodha-samāpatti*

Attainment *samādhi*: *Appanā-samādhi*

Attention (directing): *Manasikāra*

Avabodha: Understanding

Aversion: *Dosa*

Avijjā: Ignorance

Āyatanas: Our five physical sense faculties

B

Being, living: *Satta*

Bhāvanā: Meditation, meditative development

Bhikkhu: Buddhist monk

Bhikkhunī: Buddhist nun

Birth: *Jāti*

Body: *Kāya*

Boundless consciousness, state of: *Viññāṇañcāyatana*

Boundless space, state of: *Ākāsānañcāyatana*

C

Canker: *Āsava*

Cause, root: *Hetu*

Celestial beings: *Devas*

Cetanā: Volition

Chanda: Excitement of

Chena: Slash and burn farm

Citta: One mind-moment

Citt'ekaggatā: One-pointedness of mind

Clinging: *Upādāna*

Conceit: *Māna*

Concentration: *Samādhi*, one of the five spiritual faculties

Condition: *Paccaya*

Confidence: *Saddhā*, one of the five spiritual faculties

Consciousness: *Viññāṇa*

Contact, mental: *Phassa*

Conversation, ten topics to engage in: Wanting little, contentment, seclusion, aloofness from society, arousing energy, discipline, concentration, wisdom, deliverance, and knowledge and vision of deliverance

—, twenty-eight topics to avoid: Kings, robbers, ministers, armies, dangers, battles, food, drink, clothing, beds, garlands, perfumes, relatives, vehicles, villages, towns, cities, countries, women, heroes, streets, wells, the dead, trivialities, the origin of the world, the origin of the sea, whether things are so or are not so

—, expanded list of topics to avoid: In the commentaries four further kinds (of low talk) are enumerated, thus bringing the number to thirty-two, as mostly counted; namely: talk about sensuous enjoyment, self-mortification, eternity, and self-annihilation

Craving: *Taṇhā*

D

Dāna: Almsgiving

Dāyaka: Supporter

Decay and death: *Jarā-maraṇa*

Defilements, *kilesa*: Greed, aversion, delusion, conceit, speculative views, sceptical doubt, mental dullness, restlessness, shamelessness, and lack of moral dread or unconscientiousness

Delusion: *Moha*

Deva lokas: Six lower celestial worlds

Devas: Celestial beings

Dhamma: Literally: "what can be carried in the mind" also ideas, the Buddha's teachings, having the nature of, subject to, state. Generally, all kinds of phenomena

Dhātu: Elementary attitude

Diṭṭhi: View

Doing things too quickly: *Sīghaṃ*

Doing things too slowly: *Manda*

Dosa: Hatred

Doubt: *Vicikicchā*, one of five hindrances

Dukkha: Pain, painful, suffering, unease, unpleasantness

Dullness: See *Thīna-middha*

E

Effect: *Phala* (with *hetu*)

Effect of actions: *Vipāka*

Effort, mental: *Viriya*

Effort, primarily physical: *Vāyāma*

Energy: *Viriya*, one of the five spiritual faculties

Eternity view: *Sassata-diṭṭhi*

Excitement of sensual pleasures: *Kāma-cchanda*

Exerting the necessary effort: *Padhāna*

F

Feeling: *Vedanā*

Fetters: *saṃyojanas*: Personality belief, sceptical doubt, clinging to mere rules and rituals, sensual pleasure passion, ill will, fine-material passion, immaterial passion, conceit, restlessness, and ignorance.

Fine-material realm: *Rūpa-loka* corresponding to the four fine-material absorptions

Five groups of existence: See Aggregates

Five sense doors: *Pañca-dvāra*, our five internal physical sense *āyatanas*

Four great elements: *Cattāro-mahā-bhūtāṃ*

Fruit: *Phala*

Future: *Anāgata*

G

Gāthā: Verse, stanza, line of poetry

Gender: *Bhāva*

Greed: *Lobha*, *Abhijjhā*

Grief: *Domanassa*

Gross change: *Vipariṇāma*

H

Happiness: *Sukha*

Harnessing cravings: *Kappana*

Having cravings: *Icchā*

Hetu: Cause

Higher planes: The *Sugati*, the happy courses of existence-celestial, human, and the high *jhāna* states

Hindrances, the five *nīvaraṇa*: Excitement of sensual pleasures, ill will, dullness and lethargy, doubt, and restlessness and worry

Human world: *Manussa-loka*

I

Ideas: *Saṅkhāras*

Ignorance: *Avijjā*

Ill will: *Vyāpāda*, one of five hindrances

Immaterial realm: *Arūpa-loka*, *arūpāyatana*, four immaterial planes within the immaterial realm

Impermanence: *Anicca*

Imperturbable *saṇkhāra*: The fourth *jhāna* and the immaterial attainments

Indriyas, the five: See Spiritual faculties

Insubstantiality: *Anatta*, non-self

J

Jarā-maraṇa: Decay and death

Jāti: Birth

Jhāna: Mental absorptions

Jhāna-factors, the five: *Jhānanga*: one-pointedness of mind, applied thought, sustained thought, rapture, and happiness

Jhāna-samāpatti: Full attainment and control of *jhāna*; can enter the *jhāna* at will

Jīvita: Mental vitality

Joy: *Sukha*

K

Kāma-cchanda: Excitement of sensual pleasures, one of five hindrances

Kāma-loka: Sense-sphere realm

Kāma-rāga: Sensual pleasure passion

Kamma, (karma): Action

Kasiṇa: Purely external device to produce and develop concentration of mind and attain the four mental absorptions

Kāya: Body

Kilesa: See Defilements

Knowledge: *Ñāṇa*

Kosalla: Skill

Kusala: Wholesome, skilful, beneficial

Kusala-kamma: Wholesome actions

Kuṭi: Hermitage hut

L

Laziness: *Thīna-middha*

Lethargy: See *Thīna-middha*

Living being: *Satta*

Lobha: Greed

Loka: World, realm, the three realms of existence comprising the whole universe: the sense-sphere realm (*kāma-loka*), the fine-material realm (*rūpa loka*), and the immaterial realm (*arūpa loka*)

Loka, deva: Six lower celestial Worlds

Loka, peta: The realm of the departed ones, often known as the world of spirits

Lokiya: Pertaining to mundane nature

Lokuttara: Supramundane planes of liberation

Lower worlds: *Apāya*, the lower worlds

M

Magga-phala: Path and fruit

Manasikāra: Adverting; paying attention to a particular object

Mano-jīvitindriya: Mental vitality, synonymous with *nāma-jīvitindriya*

Materiality: *Rūpa*

Mental absorptions: *Jhāna*

Mental body: *Nāmakāya*

Mental effort: *Viriya*

Mentality: *Nāma*

Mentality-materiality: *Nāma-rūpa*

Mental-vitality: *Nāma-jīvitindriya, mano-jīvitindriya*

Mind: *Citta*

Mindfulness: *Sati*, one of the five spiritual faculties

Mind moment, one: *Citta*

Moha: Delusion

Morality: *Sīla*

Mundane Realms: *Lokiya*. All those states of consciousness and mental factors arising in the worldling, as well as in the noble ones, which are not associated with the supramundane (*lokuttara*)

N

Nāma: Mentality

Nāma-jīvitindriya: Mental vitality

Nāma-rūpa: Mentality-materiality

Ñāṇa: Knowledge

Neighbourhood *samādhi*: *Upacāra-samādhi*

Neither-perception-nor-non-perception, state of: *Nevasaññā-n'saññāyatana*

Nibbāna: Extinction of greed, aversion, and delusion; the third noble truth.

Nimitta: Mental reflex image gained in meditation; a totality sign

Nirodha: Cessation, extinction.

Nīvaraṇa: See Hindrances

Non-delusion: *Amoha*

Non-self: *Anatta*

Nothingness, state of: *Ākiñcaññāyatana*

Nutrient: *Āhāra*

O

Object: *Ārammaṇa*

One-pointedness of mind: *Citt'ekaggatā*

P

Paccattaṃ veditabba: Realisation by oneself

Pañca-dvāra: The five internal physical sense *āyatanas*; literally, the five sense doors

Padhāna: Exerting the necessary effort

Paññā: Wisdom

Papañca: Expansion, differentiation, proliferation

Passion, fine-material realm: *Rūpa-rāga*

Passion, immaterial realm: *Arūpa-rāga*

Passion, sensual pleasure: *Kāma-rāga*

Past: *Atīta*

Path and fruit: *Magga-phala*

Path knowledge: *Magga-ñāṇa*, a stage of enlightenment

Paṭisandhi: Re-linking consciousness

Perception: *Saññā*

Personality view: *Sakkāya-diṭṭhi*

Phala: Effect, fruit

Phassa: Mental and physical contact

Pīti: Rapture, enthusiasm

Poya day: The monthly Buddhist full moon holiday, when devout Buddhists visit a temple to hear the *Dhamma*, meditate, etc.

Pūjā: Buddhist religious service—paying homage to the Triple Gem

Pulanno: (A Sinhala word, not Pali). People who are in great need but do not beg.

Q – R

Rapture: *Pīti*

Realisation, personal: *Paccattaṃ veditabba*

Realm: See *Loka*

Recognise: *Vijānāti*

Re-linking consciousness: *Paṭisandhi*

Renewed existence, the possibility for: *Bhava*

Restlessness and worry: *Uddhacca-kukkucca*, one of the five hindrances

Results of actions: *Vipāka*

Rūpa: Materiality

Rūpa-jīvitindriya: Physical life vitality

Rūpa-loka: The fine-material realm corresponding to the four fine-material absorptions

Rūpa-rāga: Fine-material realm passion

S

Saddhā: Confidence

Sakadāgāmi: One who realises the state of once-returner and is nearly free from the fourth and fifth lower fetters

Sakkāya-diṭṭhi: Personality view

Saḷāyatana: Six sense bases

Samādhi: Concentration

Samāpatti, *jhāna*: The mind of the meditator is fully settled down in the state of *samādhi*. He or she realises all four *jhānas* and can use the *jhāna*

for many purposes, such as developing psychic powers and strengthening his or her *vipassanā*

Samatha-bhāvanā: Serenity-meditation

Saṃsāra: Rounds of birth, perpetual wandering

Saṃyojana: See Fetters

Saṅgha: Community of Buddhist monks

Saṅkhāra: Volitional formation

Saññā: Perception

Sāsana: The dispensation of the Buddha, the Buddhist teaching

Sassata-diṭṭhi: Eternity view, practising with the goal of abiding in a place where there is eternal life

Sati: Mindfulness

Satta: Living being

Self-torture: *Atta-kilamatha*

Sense-sphere realm: *Kāma-loka*

Sensual pleasure passion: *Kāma-rāga*

Sīla: Discipline; morality

Six lower celestial Worlds: *Deva lokas*

Six sense bases: *Saḷāyatana*

Skilful: *Kusala*, wholesome

Skill: *Kosalla*

Sotāpanna: One who realises the state of stream-entry and is free from the first three lower fetters

Sphere: See *Loka*

Spiritual faculties, the five *Indriyas*: Confidence, energy, mindfulness, concentration, and wisdom

Stream-entry: *Sotāpanna*

Sugati: The happy courses of existence-celestial, human, and the high *jhāna* states

Sukha: Happiness, joy

Supramundane planes of liberation: *Lokuttara*. It is a term for the eight stages of enlightenment; see also endnote 8 on page 158

Sustained thought: *Vicāra*

T

Taṇhā: Craving

Ten topics of conversation to engage in: See Conversation, topics to engage in

Thīna-middha: Laziness, dullness and lethargy, one of five hindrances

Three characteristics of existence, the: See *Tilakkhaṇa*

Tilakkhaṇa: Impermanence, suffering, and non-self; *anicca*, *dukkha* and *anatta*

Triple Gem, the: Buddha, *Dhamma*, and *Saṅgha*

Twelve causes, principle of: *Paṭiccasamuppāda*, dependent origination

Twenty-eight topics of conversation to avoid: See Conversation, topics to avoid

U

Uccheda-diṭṭhi: Annihilationist view

Uddhacca-kukkucca: Restlessness and worry, one of the five hindrances

Understanding: *Avabodha*

Unwholesome: *Akusala*

Unwholesome results: *Akusala vipāka*

Upādāna: Clinging

Upekkhā-vedanā: Neutral feeling, equanimity

V

Vedanā: Feeling

Veditabba: That which has to be realised

Vicāra: Sustained thought

Vicikicchā: Doubt, one of five hindrances

View: *Diṭṭhi*

Vihāra: Place of living, abode

Vijānāti: To know, knowing

Viññāṇa: Consciousness

Vipāka: Results of actions

Vipassanā-bhāvanā: Insight meditation

Viriya: Energy, mental effort

Vitality, physical life: *Rūpa-jīvitindriya*

Volition: *Cetanā*

Volitional formation: *Saṅkhāra*

Vyāpāda: Ill will, one of the five hindrances

W

Wholesome: *Kusala*, skilful

Wholesome actions: *Kusala-kamma*

Wholesome attention: *Yoniso-manasikāra*

Wisdom: *Paññā*, one of the five spiritual faculties

Wisdom based-on-learning: *Sutamaya-paññā*

Wisdom based-on-mental-development: *Bhāvanāmaya-paññā*

Wisdom based-on-thinking: *Cintāmaya-paññā*

X – Y – Z

Notes

1. "Strictly speaking, the word *Pāli* means text. But the expression *pāḷibhāsā,* which means language of the texts, was taken to be the name of the language itself. Its use is practically confined to Buddhist subjects, and then only in the Theravāda school." Maurice Walshe, *The Long Discourses of the Buddha: A Translation of the Dīgha Nikāya*, first Wisdom edition, (Somerville: Wisdom Publications, 1996), p. 47.
2. S.XLV.2; http://www.accesstoinsight.org/canon/sutta/saṃyutta/sn45-002.html.
3. S.VIII.4; http://www.accesstoinsight.org/canon/sutta/samyutta/sn08-004.html.
4. A.IV.85; http://www.accesstoinsight.org/canon/sutta/anguttara/an04-085.html.
5. M.31; Bhikkhu Ñāṇamoli and Bhikkhu Bodhi, *The Middle Length Discourses of the Buddha*, p. 302.
6. S.IX.11; http://www.accesstoinsight.org/canon/sutta/samyutta/sn09-011.html.
7. The three realms of the mundane sphere of existence, *lokiya*:
   * Immaterial Realm, *arūpa-loka*: (1) Sphere of Neither-Perception-Nor-Non-Perception, (2) Sphere of Nothingness, (3) Sphere of Boundless Consciousness, (4) Sphere of Boundless Space.
   * Fine-Material Realm, *rūpa-loka*: (1) Peerless *Devas*, (2) Clear-Sighted *Devas*, (3) Beautiful *Devas*, (4) Untroubled *Devas*, (5) *Devas* not Falling Away, (6) Unconscious Beings, (7) Very Fruitful *Devas*, (8) *Devas* of Resplendent Glory, (9) *Devas* of Boundless Glory, (10) *Devas* of Limited Glory, (11) *Devas* of Streaming Radiance, (12) *Devas* of Boundless Radiance, (13) *Devas* of Limited Radiance, (14) Great Brahmās (15) Ministers of Brahmā, (16) Retinue of Brahmā.
   * Sense-Sphere Realm, *kāma-loka*: (1) *Devas* Wielding Power over Others' Creations, (2) *Devas* Delighting in Creation, (3) Contented *Devas*, (4) *Yāma Devas*, (5) The Thirty-Three Gods, (6) *Devas* of the Four Great Kings, (7) Human World, (8) The Animal World, (9) The World of Hungry Ghosts, (10) The *Asuras* (Titans), and (11) The Hells.

Walshe, op. cit., pp. 38-39.

8. The four supramundane planes of liberation, *lokuttara*:
   * Fourth plane of liberation: *arahatta*. One realises the fruit of holiness and is free from the five lower and five higher fetters (see glossary).
   * Third plane of liberation: *anāgāmi*. One realises the fruit of non-returner and is fully free from the first five lower fetters.
   * Second plane of liberation: *sakadāgāmi*. One realises the fruit of once-returner and is nearly free from the fourth and fifth lower fetters.
   * First plane of liberation: *sotāpatti.* One realises the fruit of stream-entry and is free from the first three lower fetters.

From Nyanatiloka Thera, *Buddhist Dictionary: Manual of Buddhist Terms and Doctrines*, fourth revised edition, Kandy: BPS, 1980, p. 24.

9. Sn. Verse 2; http://www.accesstoinsight.org/canon/sutta/khuddaka/suttanipata/snp5-02.html.

10. S. LVI.11; http://www.accesstoinsight.org/canon/sutta/samyutta/sn56-011a.html.

11. D.22; trans. in Walshe, *op. cit.*, p. 346 (adapted).

12. Dh. Verse 23; http://www.metta.lk/tipitaka/2Sutta-Pitaka/5Khuddaka-Nikaya/02Dhammapada/02-Appamadavaggo-e1.html

13. M.4; trans. in Ñāṇamoli and Bodhi, *op. cit.*, p. 105.

14. A.III.40; http://www.accesstoinsight.org/canon/sutta/anguttara/an03-040.html.

15. M.9; trans. in Ñāṇamoli and Bodhi, *op. cit.*, p. 132.

16. S.XXII.79; http://www.accesstoinsight.org/canon/sutta/samyutta/sn22-079.html.

17. M.123; trans. in Ñāṇamoli and Bodhi, *op. cit.,* p. 983.

18. M.14; trans. in Ñāṇamoli and Bodhi, *op. cit.*, p. 187.

19. D.8; trans. in Walshe, *op. cit.*, p. 156.

20. M.31; trans. in Ñāṇamoli and Bodhi, *op. cit.*, p. 302.

21. M.10; trans. in Ñāṇamoli and Bodhi, *op. cit.*, p. 145.

22. A. X. 26; http://www.accesstoinsight.org/lib/bps/wheels/wheel405.html#ch6.